The Life of Christ

Lucian Farrar, Jr.

James Kay Publishing

Tulsa, Oklahoma

The Life of Christ
ISBN 978-1-943245-64-2

www.jameskaypublishing.com

e-mail: sales@jameskaypublishing.com

© 2021 Lucian Farrar, Jr.
Cover design by JKP
Author Photo by Bob Cooper

All rights reserved.
No part of this book may be reproduced in any form or by any means
- except for review questions and brief quotations -
without permission in writing from the author.

also by
Lucian Farrar, Jr.

The Victorious Church
In the Book of Revelation
A Commentary and Questions

The Book of Daniel
The Most High Rules
A Commentary and Questions

The Book of Isaiah
Christ, Our Redeemer
A Commentary and Questions

The Minor Prophets
God's Spokesmen
A Commentary and Questions

Psalms – Book 1
David's Original Collection

The King James Version is used with archaic words, word order, and punctuations replaced by those that are in current use.

Other translations are used to replace archaic words with those that can be understood today or to give a more accurate meaning of the original text. These abbreviations acknowledge the translations:

ESV – English Standard Version
NASB – New American Standard Version, 1973 Edition
NIV – New International Version, 1996 Edition
NKJV – New King James Version.

Dedication

This book is dedicated to my third son

Lucian Mark Farrar

After teaching at Greater Tulsa Christian Academy, Mark served as an associate minister for the Crosstown Church of Christ in Tulsa, Oklahoma. He then became the pulpit minister for the Downtown Church of Christ in Bixby, Oklahoma, and he later served the Seventh & Mueller Church of Christ in Paragould, Arkansas in the same capacity. At the time of this writing, he is an instructor at Tulsa Tech, teaching mathematics.

While working on his M.A. degree in Ministry at Oklahoma Christian, among the courses he enjoyed was The Life of Christ. Mark has always sought to emphasize Jesus Christ in his teaching and preaching. It is my desire that in the future, he will have the opportunity to add his understanding and thoughts on the life of Christ to this book.

— Lucian Farrar, Jr.

Thank You

A word of thanks to Bob Colvin for his time in proofreading this manuscript.

Table of Contents

Dedication ix

The Life of Christ 1

Preparation for Christ's Ministry 13

The Beginning of Christ's Ministry 25

The Early Ministry in Galilee 33

Growing Popularity and Opposition 37

Jesus Instructs His Apostles 47

The Great Power of Jesus 57

The Year of Opposition 67

The Ministry in Judea 77

The Ministry in Perea 89

Jesus Returns to Bethany 103

The Journey for the Passover 107

The Last Week 113

The Last Supper 129

Wednesday Evening 137

The Trials 147

The Crucifixion and Burial 155

The Resurrection and Ascension 161

The Life of Christ

The purpose of Christ's earthly ministry was to make an atoning sacrifice of himself for our sins and to establish a spiritual kingdom. God "has blessed us with all spiritual blessings in the heavenly *places* in Christ." (Ephesians 1:3) The writings of Matthew, Mark, Luke, and John are called the four gospels, because they report the good news of the life of Christ. After teaching us the way to live, he died for our sins, and he rose from the dead. He now is reigning in heaven and providing forgiveness and eternal life for us.

At first, there was no need for written accounts of what Jesus had said and done. Ralph Earle explains, "The vivid account of the eyewitness was preferred to the more impersonal written record." [1] Matthew and John were eye-witnesses and his apostles. Mark was closely associated with the apostle Peter, another eyewitness. (1 Peter 5:13) Luke, as an inspired historian, used the testimonies of eyewitnesses. The Holy Spirit enabled these writers to remember the things that Jesus had said and done. Jesus had promised that the Holy Spirit would teach them all things and to bring all things to their remembrance what he had said. (John 14:26) Therefore, we should not be surprised that the writers would agree, using the very same words at times.

But how can differences be explained? The ministry of Jesus was a period of three and a half years, over 1200 days, but "only about fifty days of Jesus' ministry are touched upon in the combined Gospels." [2] Merrill Tenney points out, "The Gospels themselves do not claim to be exhaustive accounts of all that Jesus said or

---

[1] Ralph Earle, *Exploring the New Testament*, p. 64
[2] Bruce Wilkinson & Kenneth Boa, *Talk Thru the Bible*, p. 303

did," and "each Gospel was selective according to the purpose of the author." [3] Jesus spoke on the same subject at different times and at various places, but he used different words and illustrations, much like preachers and teachers do today. Matthew's account of the Sermon on the Mount, while being similar to Luke's account of the Sermon on the Level Place, was at a different place and time. Even when writing about the same event, Matthew could accurately report one thing, and Luke could mention another.

All four Gospels emphasize the closing days of Jesus' ministry. From his Triumphal Entry into Jerusalem on the Sunday before his crucifixion to his ascension into Heaven, Matthew uses eight chapters; Mark uses six chapters; Luke uses five-and-a-half chapters; and John takes ten chapters to cover this last period. The Triumphal Entry was one week before Jesus' resurrection from the dead, and he ascended into heaven forty days after being raised. (Acts 1:1-3) That was only 47 days.

Four Portraits of Jesus

Matthew pictures Jesus as the Christ, the King who fulfilled the messianic prophecies. **Mark** shows him as the Conqueror in the days of the Romans. **Luke** reveals Jesus as the Savior for all. **John** pictures Jesus as God in the flesh. Events and teachings from the life of Jesus are arranged in order to portray him according to the theme of each book. The four Gospels are not attempting to give a complete chronological biography of the life of Christ.

However, this study is an attempt to see the life of Christ in its chronological order as far as possible. First of all, we want to look at the four gospels in the order in which they were written.

---

[3] Merrill C. Tenney, *New Testament Survey*, p. 133; John 20:30, 21:25

MARK

The Conqueror in the Days of the Romans

Although "the present order of the four Gospels goes back to at least the late second century," [4] many scholars now believe that the gospel according to Mark was the first to have been written.[5] About AD 115, Papias, an elder of the church in Hierapolis (Colossians 4:13), connected the Gospel of Mark with the preaching of Peter in Rome.[6] He said, "Mark became Peter's interpreter and wrote down accurately, but not in the order, all that he remembered of the things said and done by the Lord." [7] As the "interpreter of Peter," Mark translated Peter's messages into Greek, the language in which the Gospel according to Mark is written. The date was about AD 63.

Eusebius relates the following story by Clement of Alexandria (c. AD 180): "Peter's hearers, not satisfied with a single hearing or with the unwritten teaching of the divine message, pleaded with Mark, whose Gospel we have, to leave them a written summary of the teaching given them verbally, since he was a follower of Peter. Nor did they cease until they persuaded him and so caused the writing of what is called the Gospel according to Mark." Eusebius says, "Clement quotes this story in *Outlines*, Book 6 ... He also points out that Peter mentions Mark in his first epistle and that he composed this in Rome, which they say he indicates when referring to the city figuratively as Babylon in the words, 'Your sister church in Babylon, chosen together with you, sends you greetings; and so does my son Mark' (1 Peter 5:13)." [8]

---

[4] Bruce Wilkinson & Kenneth Boa, *Talk Thru the Bible*, p. 303
[5] Ibid., p. 319
[6] Merrill C. Tenney, *New Testament Survey*, p. 155
[7] Paul L. Maier, *Eusebius – The Church History*, Book 3, 39, p. 129
[8] Paul L. Maier, *Eusebius – The Church History*, Book 2, 15, p. 73

Notice these three things: (1) The other Gospels were not in circulation; the Christians in Rome did not have a written Gospel to read before Mark wrote his account. (2) At that time, the need in Rome for a written gospel was greater than in Palestine where more eyewitnesses of Christ were still living. (3) Mark wrote his Gospel in Rome for the Romans. Wilkinson and Boa conclude: "This may be why Mark omitted a number of items that would not have been meaningful to Gentiles, such as the genealogy of Christ, fulfilled prophecy, references to the Law, and certain Jewish customs that are found in other gospels. Mark interpreted Aramaic words (3:17; 5:41; 7:34; 15:22)."[9] Merrill Tenney observes, "There are many Latinisms in Mark, such as *modius* for 'bushel' (4:21), *census* for "tribute" (12:14), *speculator* for "executioner" (6:27), *centurio* for 'centurion' (15:39, 44, 45) and others. For the most of these there were Greek equivalents. Mark apparently used the Latin terms because they were more familiar. The Gospel contains little emphasis on Jewish law and customs. When they are mentioned, they are explained more fully than in the other Synoptics." [10]

We know that Mark was in Rome with Paul during his first imprisonment, when the apostle wrote letters to the Colossians and to Philemon.[11] As a prisoner in Rome awaiting his execution, Paul sent for Mark, saying, "He is useful to me for ministry." [12]

Mark reveals the Conqueror who set up the kingdom of God in the days of the Roman Empire. He mentions "the kingdom of God" fifteen times in his account.

Jesus preached, "The time is fulfilled, and the kingdom of God is at hand." (Mark 1:15) Jesus fulfilled

---

[9] Bruce Wilkinson & Kenneth Boa, *Talk Thru the Bible*, p. 320
[10] Merrill C. Tenney, *New Testament Survey*, p. 157
[11] Colossians 4:10, Philemon 24
[12] 2 Timothy 4:11

the prophecy in Daniel 2:44 that in the days of the Roman kings, the God of heaven would set up a kingdom that would never be destroyed. Jesus promised, "There are some of them that stand here, which shall not taste of death, till they have seen the kingdom of God come with power." (Mark 9:1) From the city of Rome, the seat of the Roman Empire, Mark proclaims the gospel of Jesus Christ.

The writer's full name is John Mark. John is a Hebrew name; Mark is Latin. Mark's mother had a large house in Jerusalem where the church met to pray for Peter while in prison. (Acts 12:12-17) He is called "John" in Acts 13, verses 5 and 13, but he is known as "Mark" after going with Barnabas to Cyprus for mission work. (Acts 15:37) He and Barnabas were cousins, according to Colossians 4:10. Peter's reference to Mark as "my son" in 1 Peter 5:13 indicates Peter was the one who led Mark to Christ.

The key word in Mark is *immediately*; it is used 40 times. Mark rapidly reveals Jesus as the Conqueror over temptations (Mark 1:12-13), over occupations (1:16-20), over unclean spirits (1:21-28), over sicknesses (1:29-34), over leprosy (1:40-45), over sins (2:1-12), over social prejudices (2:13-17), over religious prejudices (2:23 – 3:6), over death (8:31; 16:6), over blindness (10:46-52), over enemies (12:13-17), over ignorance (12:18-27), and over false prophets (13:21-27). As world Conqueror, Jesus ordered his followers, "Go ye into all the world and preach the gospel to every creature. He that believes and is baptized shall be saved; but he that believes not shall be damned." (16:15) In Daniel's prophecy, the kingdom of God is represented by a mountain that filled the whole earth. (Daniel 2:34-35, 44-45)

MATTHEW

Jesus Is the Christ, the King

Jesus is the Messiah that the Jews were expecting to reign on David's throne. He is Immanuel, "God with us" (1:23), fulfilling Isaiah 7:14. Jesus is "the Christ, the Son of the living God." (16:16) He has all power and authority in heaven and on earth. (28:18) Eleven times Matthew appeals to the Old Testament Scriptures, saying, "that it might be fulfilled" or "then was fulfilled".

Matthew's gospel was for the Gentiles as well as the Jews. He reports the Great Commission saying, "Go ye therefore, and teach all nations." (28:19) Matthew wrote his account in Greek, the universal language, to reveal that Jesus came to bless all nations. Christ fulfills the promise made to Abraham, "And in your seed shall all the nations of the earth be blessed." (Genesis 22:18)

Matthew had been a tax collector for the Roman government in the city of Capernaum before being called by Jesus to be an apostle. (Matthew 9:9) He appears to have been an educated man who was in the habit of taking notes as part of his business activities. "The early church uniformly attributed this gospel to Matthew, and no tradition to the contrary ever emerged." [13] Many today believe that Matthew depended on Mark's gospel as a source, but he had additional information to report with a different emphasis. Being an apostle of Christ, Matthew was inspired to remember all things that Jesus had said. (John 14:26)

Matthew's account appears first in the New Testament because he shows that Jesus fulfilled Old Testament prophecies about the Christ and his kingdom.

---

[13] Wilkinson & Boa, *Talk Thru the Bible*, p. 308

LUKE

The Savior for All Mankind

"For the Son of man is come to seek and to save that which was lost." Luke 19:10

Jesus Christ is the Savior for all classes of people. An angel announced his birth, saying, "There is born to you ... a Savior, who is Christ the Lord." [14] While holding the baby Jesus in his arms, the prophet Simeon praised God, saying, "Mine eyes have seen your salvation, which you have prepared before the face of all people, a light to lighten the Gentiles, and the glory of your people Israel." (2:25-32) Jesus showed his power to forgive sins; Luke tells of his forgiving a paralytic man, a sinful woman, a tax collector, and a criminal.[15] Jesus declared "that repentance and remission of sins should be preached in his name to all nations." (24:47) Luke portrays Jesus Christ as the perfect Son of Man who has compassion for sinners, hope for the poor, and respect for women. He is the Savior for all.

Luke was closely associated with Paul, an apostle to the Gentiles.[16] He was with Paul during his first imprisonment in Rome, where Paul calls Luke "the beloved physician" in Colossians 4:14 and "my fellow laborer" in Philemon 24. During Paul's second imprisonment in Rome, just prior to his execution, Paul wrote, "Only Luke is with me." (2 Tim. 4:11) As a physician, Luke would have been well-educated, and this is seen in his superb writing ability in the Greek language. As a writer of Holy Scripture, he also was inspired by the Holy Spirit. Luke was a Gentile convert. He is listed in Colossians 4:10-14 with Paul's fellow workers who were not "of the circumcision"—those that were not Jews. According to early church tradition,

---

[14] Luke 2:11
[15] Luke 5:17, Luke 7:36-50, Luke 19:8-10, Luke 23:39-43
[16] Romans 11:13, "we" in Acts 16:1:17; 20:5 – 21:18; 27:1 – 28:16

Luke was from Syrian Antioch, remained unmarried, and died at the age of eighty-four.[17]

Luke addresses his account of the gospel of Christ to a man named Theophilus, meaning "friend of God." (1:1-4) Luke calls him **"most excellent"**, which is a title of an official of high rank.[18] He appears to have been a recent Gentile convert seeking confirmation of the things he had learned. Luke tells his story of the life of Jesus in the context of the Roman emperors Augustus and Tiberius. As a good historian, Luke gathered the testimony of written sources and of eyewitnesses, including the apostles. Important information needed to be added to both Mark and Matthew's accounts.

---

[17] Wilkinson & Boa, *Talk Thru the Bible,* p. 327
[18] Acts 23:26, Acts 26:25

JOHN
Jesus was God in the Flesh

John wrote the fourth Gospel about the year AD 100 in the city of Ephesus, after writing Revelation. The Anti-Marcionite Prologues, written in the middle of the second century, state: "John the apostle, one of the Twelve, wrote the Apocalypse on the Island of Patmos, and after that the Gospel." [19] Jesus' divine nature is emphasized by John.

"In the beginning was the Word, and the Word was with God and **the Word was God**. ... All things were made by him, and without him was not anything made that was made. **And the Word was made flesh** and dwelt among us; and we beheld his glory." (John 1:1-3,14)

John records seven **"I am"** statements of Jesus. He said, "I am the bread of life" in 6:35; "I am the good shepherd" in 10:11; "I am the resurrection and the life" in 11:25; "I am the way, the truth, and the life" in 14:6; "I am the true vine" in 15:1; "If ye believe not that **I AM**, ye shall die in your sins" in 8:24; and in 8:58 he said, "I say to you, before Abraham was **I AM**." God is the great **"I AM"** in Exodus 3:14. He is the eternal existing One.

To prove these claims of Jesus, John records seven miraculous signs. Jesus turned water into wine. (2:1-11) Jesus healed the nobleman's son at a distance. (4:46-54) Jesus healed an invalid man at the Pool of Bethesda. (5:1-15) Jesus multiplied five loaves and two small fish and fed five thousand men. (6:1-10) Jesus walked on the water of the sea. (6:15-21) Jesus gave sight to a man born blind. (9:1-11) And Jesus raised Lazarus, who had been dead for four days. (11:1-44)

---

[19] J. W. Roberts, *The Letters of John*, p. 11

John writes, "And many other signs truly did Jesus in the presence of his disciples, which are not written in this book; but these are written that ye might believe that Jesus is the Christ, the Son of God; and that believing ye might have life through his name." (20:30-31)

Suggestions for Reading the Life of Christ

Read first the comments for each section. You will get more out of this study if you will read all of the Scripture references in the comments. Then read all the Scriptures under the section headings in the order that they are given.

Review Questions

1. Why did Christ come to earth? _____
   _____
   _____

2. What is the "good news" of Christ's earthly ministry?
   _____
   _____
   _____
   _____

3. The ministry of Jesus was how long? _____

4. About how many days of Jesus' ministry are covered in the combined four Gospels? _____

5. All four Gospels emphasize the _____ _____ of Jesus' ministry.

6. How does Matthew picture Christ?
   _____

7. How does Mark picture Christ?
   _____

8. How does Luke picture Christ?
   _____

9. How does John picture Christ?
   _____

10. These four Gospels are not attempting to give a complete _____ _____ of the life of Jesus.

11. Which one of the four Gospels appears to have been the first to have been written? _____

12. Which Gospel reveals that Jesus fulfilled Isaiah's prophecy of the coming of Immanuel, "God with us."
_____

13. Which writer was closely associated with Peter?
_____

14. Which writer was closely associated with Paul?
_____

15. Which writer refers to Jesus as "the Word," who was with God in the beginning? _____

16. John wrote the fourth Gospel about the year AD ___ in city of Ephesus, after writing _____.

Preparations for Christ's Ministry

Christ's Work before He Became Flesh
John 1:1-18

Before he became the Son of God in the flesh, Christ existed in eternity as the Word of God. He is the spokesman for the one Godhead; and that is why, he is called the Word. He was involved in the creation of all things. (Colossians 1:16-18)

He appears in the Old Testament as The Angel of God. The word **angel** means "messenger." Whenever God spoke to man, it was the Word speaking. The Angel of the LORD spoke to Abraham in Genesis 22:15-18, saying "And in thy seed shall all the nations of the earth be blessed." The Angel of the LORD spoke to Moses at the burning bush in Exodus 3:2-14. He is the LORD, the great I AM.

The Genealogy of Jesus Christ
Matthew 1:1-17; Luke 3:23-38

Matthew's account begins with the genealogy of Jesus. He starts with Abraham, Isaac, and Jacob and concludes with "Joseph the husband of Mary, of whom was born Jesus." (1:16) Among Jesus' ancestors were two Gentile women: Rahab the Canaanite and Ruth the Moabite. (1:5) Also, there were two women that are remembered for their sins: Tamar (1:3) and Bathsheba, who had been the wife of Uriah. (1:6) Christ came to provide salvation for sinners of all nations. Matthew lists 42 generations and divides them into three groups of 14 each. (1:17)

Luke's genealogy of Christ begins with Jesus and traces it all the way back to "Adam, which was the son of God." (3:38) Christ is the Son of God for all mankind.

Matthew gives the legal genealogy through Joseph, and Luke gives the genealogy through Mary. Both genealogies prove that Jesus was a descendent of King David, through whom the Christ was to come.

The Coming of John the Baptist
Luke 1:5-25

Luke's account begins with the story of a priest named Zacharias and his wife Elizabeth, who lived in the days of Herod the Great, king of Judea. Although they were righteous before God, they had no child, and they were getting old. The angel Gabriel appeared to Zacharias as he was standing by the altar of incense in the temple. He told the priest that he and his wife Elizabeth would have a son, and they were to name him John. Being filled with the Holy Spirit, John would turn many of the children of Israel back to the Lord their God. He would be like Elijah the prophet, causing God's people to repent. He would prepare the people for the coming of Christ, fulfilling the prophecies of Malachi 3:1 and Malachi 4:5-6, the closing verses of the Old Testament. When Zacharias asked for a sign that this message was from God, the angel said that he would not be able to speak until the child was born.

The Angel Gabriel Appears to Mary
Luke 1:26-38

In the sixth month of Elizabeth's pregnancy, God sent the angel Gabriel to the city of Nazareth to a virgin named Mary. He said to her, "Fear not, Mary, for you have found favor with God. And behold, you shall conceive in your womb and bring forth a son, and you shall call his name JESUS. He shall be called the Son of the Highest. And the Lord God shall give to him the throne of his father David, and he shall reign over the house of Jacob forever; and of his kingdom there will be no end." Mary had not known a man in a sexual way, so she said to the angel, "How shall this be?" And the angel answered her, "The Holy Spirit shall come upon you, and the power of the Highest shall overshadow you." She would give birth to the Son of God. Gabriel told Mary that her cousin Elizabeth had conceived a son in her old age; and he said, "For with God nothing shall be impossible." Mary said, "Behold the handmaid of the Lord; be it unto me according to your word."

Gabriel, who appeared to Mary, is the same angel who revealed to Daniel the vision of the seventieth week, in which the Messiah would come "to make an end of sins, to make reconciliation for iniquity," and "to bring in everlasting righteousness." (Daniel 9:21-27) The nature of Christ's kingdom would be spiritual.

Mary Visits Elizabeth
Luke 1:39-45

Mary went to a city in Judah to visit her relative Elizabeth, who was filled with the Holy Spirit and prophesied, saying, "Blessed are you among women, and blessed is the fruit of your womb! And why is this granted to me that the mother of my Lord should come to me? For behold, when the sound of your greeting came to my ears, the baby in my womb leaped for joy. And blessed is she who believed that there would be a fulfillment of what was spoken to her from the Lord." ESV

Mary's Song of Praise
Luke 1:46-56

Mary praised God saying, "My soul magnifies the Lord, and my spirit has rejoiced in God my Savior. For he has regarded the low estate of his handmaiden. For behold, from now on all generations shall call me blessed. For he that is mighty has done to me great things; and holy is his name. And his mercy is on them that fear him from generation to generation." Mary stayed with Elizabeth about three months before returning to Nazareth. She probably stayed until John was born.

The Birth of John the Baptist
Luke 1:57-66

When Elizabeth gave birth to a son, neighbors and relatives came and rejoiced with her. They all thought that he would be named after his aged father, Zacharias, but Elizabeth said, "Not so; but he shall be called John." They objected, because no one in their family had been called by that name. Then Zacharias using sign language requested a writing tablet, and he wrote, "His name is John." Immediately, Zacharias was able to speak and praise God.

The Prophecy of Zacharias
Luke 1:67-79

"Blessed be the Lord God of Israel, for he has visited and redeemed his people and has raised up a horn of salvation for us in the house of his servant David ... And you, child, shall be called the prophet of the Highest; for you shall go before the face of the Lord to prepare his ways, to give knowledge of salvation unto his people by the remission of their sins, through the tender mercy of our God, whereby the dayspring from on high has visited us to give light to them that sit in darkness and in the shadow of death, to guide our feet into the way of peace." The sunrise, **"the dayspring**," is a reference to Malachi 4:2, which says, "The Sun of Righteousness shall arise with healing in His wings." NKJV Christ would give light to those who sit in darkness and in the shadow of death, fulfilling the prophecy of Isaiah 9:2.

The Birth of Jesus
Matthew 1:18-25; Luke 2:1-7

Matthew relates how an angel assured Joseph that the child conceived by Mary was of the Holy Spirit. He told Joseph to call her son JESUS, "for he shall save his people from their sins." Matthew says, "All this was done, that it might be fulfilled which was spoken of the Lord by the prophet." The apostle then quotes Isaiah 7:14

that predicts the virgin birth of "Immanuel" whose name means "God with us." Mary remained a virgin until she had given birth to her firstborn son, and they called his name Jesus.

Luke tells us that Jesus was born during the reign of Caesar Augustus. As the first Roman emperor, Augustus issued an imperial decree for a census to be taken throughout the entire Roman Empire. Joseph, being a descendant of David, had to return to the city of Bethlehem, his ancestral home. Before Joseph and Mary made this trip of eighty miles from Nazareth to Bethlehem, Joseph had taken Mary to be is wife. Luke uses the word **betrothed** (espoused, KJV), because they had not yet consummated their relationship, according to Matthew 1:25. Because there was no room for them in the inn, Jesus was born in a stable and was wrapped in swaddling clothes and laid in a manger, which is a feeding trough for livestock.

Angels Announce Christ's Birth
Luke 2:8-20

As shepherds were watching over their flocks at night, an angel appeared to them with this announcement: "Fear not! For behold, I bring you good tidings of great joy, which shall be to all people. For unto you is born this day in the city of David a Savior, who is Christ the Lord." The angel gave them a sign: they would find the baby lying in a manger. Then suddenly there was a multitude of angels praising God and saying, "Glory to God in the highest, and on earth peace, good will toward men." The shepherds went with haste into the city and found the baby lying in a manger. And the shepherds praised God for all the things that they had seen and heard. Mary kept all these things in her heart and thought about them often. As an eyewitness, Mary may have been one of Luke's sources of information. Luke may have also interviewed the shepherds, for they were "glorifying and praising God for all the things that they had heard and seen."

The Baby is Named Jesus
Luke 2:21

As Mary and Joseph were instructed by angels, the baby was named Jesus at the time of his circumcision on the eighth day, according to the law in Leviticus 12:2-3.

Jesus Is Presented at the Temple
Luke 2:22-39

Forty days after his birth, Jesus was presented in the temple as the firstborn son of Mary. They made a sacrifice of birds instead of a lamb, in keeping with the law for the poor in Leviticus 12:2-8. The prophet Simeon praised God for letting him see the Christ child, and he predicted that Christ would suffer by saying to Mary, "a sword shall pierce through your own soul also." Anna, an eighty-four-year-old prophetess, gave thanks to God for Jesus, and she spoke of him to all that were looking for redemption. Mary and Joseph performed all things according to the law.

The Visit of the Wise Men from the East
Matthew 2:1-12

Wise men from the East came to Jerusalem, asking, "Where is he that is born King of the Jews?" When it was inquired where the Christ was to be born, the answer was given: "In Bethlehem of Judea, for thus it is written by the prophet." Then they read the prophecy of Micah 5:2. When the wise men came into **the house** (not the stable), they saw the young **child** and worshiped him presenting gifts of gold, frankincense, and myrrh. Being warned by God, they did not return to Herod, who had pretended that he wanted to worship Jesus; but they departed to their own country another way.

The Flight into Egypt
Matthew 2:13-18

An angel of God instructed Joseph in a dream to take the young child to Egypt, because Herod was seeking to destroy him. They left by night for Egypt and stayed there until the death of Herod. This fulfilled the prophecy of Hosea 11:1, "Out of Egypt I have called my son." In an effort to kill Jesus, Herod sent his soldiers to Bethlehem and the surrounding area to kill all the male children from two years old and under. This massacre fulfilled the typical prophecy of Jeremiah 31:15.

Jesus' Home in Nazareth
Matthew 2:19-23; Luke 2:39-40

When Herod was dead, Joseph took the young child Jesus and his mother back to the land of Israel, and they went into Galilee and made their home in Nazareth, "that it might be fulfilled which was spoken by the prophets, He shall be called a Nazarene." This is not a reference to any particular quotation but to the general description of the Messiah being despised, as in Isaiah 53:2-3 and Psalm 22:6. Nazareth was an insignificant small town with a mixed population in the hills of Galilee. When Nathanael first heard of Jesus, he asked rhetorically, "Can any good thing come out of Nazareth?" (John 1:46) The word Nazarene means an inhabitant of Nazareth, and it is used many times to refer to Jesus. "Jesus the Nazarene" is translated "Jesus from Nazareth" and "Jesus of Nazareth." Christ was indeed "a root out of dry ground." He was "despised and rejected of men;" but "with his stripes we are healed," because "the LORD has laid on him the iniquity of us all." (Isaiah 53:2- 6) His followers are called "the sect of the Nazarenes" by the Jewish leaders in Acts 24:5.

Luke omits the visit of the wise men and the flight to Egypt, because these events do not fit his portrait of Jesus as Savior. The story of the wise men seeking to find the King of the Jews serves well Matthew's portrait of Jesus as Christ the King. Matthew takes an entire chapter to tell the stories of the wise men and of Jesus going to Egypt. Luke had nothing to add to this narrative. So, he goes from the presentation of Jesus in Jerusalem to the return of the family to Nazareth, where "the child grew and became strong in spirit, filled with wisdom, and the grace of God was upon him." (Luke 2:39-40)

Jesus at Age Twelve
Luke 2:41-52

After attending the Feast of the Passover in Jerusalem when Jesus was twelve years old, Joseph and Mary went a day's journey before realizing that Jesus was not with them. On the third day they found him in the temple in the midst of the teachers, both listening to them and asking questions. All who heard him were surprised at his understanding. When his parents found him, Jesus said to them, "Did you not know that I must be about my Father's business?" These are the first recorded words of Jesus. Even at this young age, Jesus was aware of his Father in heaven, who had work for him to do. However, Jesus set the perfect example for young people as they grow into maturity. After impressing the scholars in the temple, young Jesus went with his parents to their home in Nazareth and was subject to them. "And Jesus increased in wisdom and stature, and in favor with God and man."

The Early Life of John the Baptist
Luke 1:80

"And the child grew and became strong in spirit, and was in the deserts till the day of his showing to Israel." This verse covers a period of about thirty years. His elderly parents had likely died. He may have been in the deserts preparing for his ministry. (cp. Paul in Arabia, Gal. 1:17)

John the Baptist Begins Preaching
Luke 3:1-18; John 1:6-7, 15-18, 23;
Mark 1:2-8; Matthew 3:1-12

Luke gives the historical setting. John began his ministry in the fifteenth year of Tiberius Caesar, when Pontius Pilate was governor of Judea and Herod [Antipas] was tetrarch of Galilee and Perea. Tiberius was the Roman emperor from AD 14 to 37; this period included the church's beginning. Luke introduces the work of John by quoting the prophecy of Isaiah 40:3-5, which ends with these words: "All flesh shall see the salvation of God." Luke includes John's instructions to the people concerning giving; to the tax collectors to collect no more than what is due; and to the soldiers to refrain from intimidations and false accusations and to be content with their wages.

All four gospels quote Isaiah 40:3, "The voice of one crying in the wilderness, 'Prepare the way of the LORD.'" Only Mark refers to Malachi 3:1, "Behold, I send my messenger before thy face, who shall prepare thy way before thee."

Mark and Matthew report on John's clothing of camel's hair and his diet of locust and wild honey. All three synoptic gospels mention John's preaching the baptism of repentance and saying that a mightier One was coming who would baptize with the Holy Spirit.

Both Matthew and Luke tell of the multitudes that came to be baptized, but John the Baptist instructed them to "bring forth therefore fruits worthy of repentance." (Luke 3:8; Matthew 3:8) These two gospels also record John's blessing that the wheat would be gathered into the barn and his warning that the chaff would be burned up with unquenchable fire. (Matthew 3:12; Luke 3:17)

John Baptizes Jesus
Matthew 3:13-17; Mark 1:9-11; Luke 3:21-22

Jesus came from Galilee to be baptized by John in the Jordan river. At first, John refused to baptize Jesus, saying, "I need to be baptized of you, and do you come to me?" But Jesus said to him, "Allow it to be so now; for thus it becomes us to fulfill all righteousness."

Then John baptized Jesus. When Jesus came up out of the water, the Holy Spirit of God descended upon him, and a voice from heaven said, "This is my beloved Son, in whom I am well pleased." The three persons in the one Godhead are clearly seen here. God the Father is speaking from heaven; God the Son is coming up out of the water, and the Holy Spirit of God is descending upon him. Luke says Jesus was praying when the heaven was opened.

The Temptations of Jesus
Luke 4:1-13; Matthew 4:1-11; Mark 1:12-13

Then Jesus, being full of the Holy Spirit's power, was led by the Spirit into the wilderness to be tempted for forty days by the devil. Matthew and Luke add that Jesus was fasting during this time. Matthew relates the last three temptations in chronological order. After the third one, he says, "**Then** the devil left him." Luke arranges the temptations in topical order: turning stones into bread (the lust of the flesh), showing him all the kingdoms of the world that could be his (the lust of the eyes), and jumping off the pinnacle of the temple and having the angels to bear him up (the pride of life). Eve had been tempted in these three ways. (Genesis 3:6) Jesus overcame each temptation by quoting the written word of God. "And when the devil had ended every temptation, he departed him until an opportune time." ESV (Luke 4:13)

The Identity of John the Baptist
John 1:19-28

When the people heard John's preaching, they were filled with expectation, and they wondered if John were the Christ. (Luke 3:15) The Jews sent priests and Levites to ask John, "Who are you?" He confessed, "I am not the Christ." Then they asked, "Are you Elijah?" (Malachi 4:5) And he replied, "I am not." John came in the spirit and power of Elijah (Luke 1:17), but he was not Elijah reincarnated as some thought. They asked, "Are you the Prophet?" Was John the prophet that would be like Moses? (Deut. 18:15-19) John answered, "No." Again they asked, "Who are you?" John said, "I am the voice of one crying in the wilderness, 'Make straight the way of the Lord,' as said by the prophet Isaiah." He was fulfilling the prophecy of Isaiah 40:3, which says, "The voice of him that cries, in the wilderness, 'Prepare the way of the LORD, make straight in the desert a highway for our God.'" Isaiah had predicted that the eternal God would be coming in the flesh. Had the Jews studied their own prophets they would have never convicted Jesus of blasphemy. Christ would be eternal divinity. John was preparing the way for God to come into the world. This questioning of John occurred on the other side of the Jordan river, where he was baptizing.

John Introduces Jesus
John 1:29-34

The next day, John introduced Jesus to the people, saying, "Behold the Lamb of God, who takes away the sin of the world." John said that Jesus is "preferred before me; for he was before me." John was six months older than Jesus, but Jesus was before him as an eternal divine being. God had revealed a sign to John that upon whom he would see the Spirit descending and remaining, he would be the One, who baptizes with the Holy Spirit. John said that he saw the Spirit descending from heaven like a dove and remaining on Jesus. This sign was infallible proof to John that Jesus is the Son of God. Jesus was about thirty years of age when he began his ministry, according to Luke 3:23.

The Beginning of Christ's Ministry

The First Disciples of Jesus
John 1:35-42

The day after John the Baptist had introduced Jesus as "The Lamb of God," two of his disciples began following Jesus. He turned and asked, "What do you seek?" They answered, "Rabbi (meaning, Teacher), where are you staying?" He said, "Come and see." Andrew was one of the two disciples (verse 40); the other one is not named. John never mentions himself by name in his writings. And since the writer notes that it was about the tenth hour when they came to where Jesus was staying, the other disciple must have been John. Our four o'clock in the afternoon would have been their tenth hour. Andrew then found his brother Simon and said to him, "We have found the Messiah!" And he brought him to Jesus. When Jesus saw Simon, he said, "You shall be called Cephas." Cephas is the Aramaic word for Peter, meaning a stone or rock. Peter, Andrew, and John spent the rest of the day with Jesus. These three were the first disciples of Jesus.

Philip and Nathanael Become Disciples
John 1:43-51

The following day, as Jesus prepared to go into Galilee, he called Philip to be one of his disciples. Philip was from Bethsaida, a city near Capernaum, which was in Galilee. Andrew and Peter also were from Bethsaida originally; they likely were acquainted.

Then Philip found Nathanael and told him about Jesus of Nazareth, who was fulfilling the writings of Moses and the prophets. Nathanael asked, "Can there any good thing come out of Nazareth?" His rhetorical question proves that Jesus fulfilled what Isaiah had written about the Christ, saying, "He shall grow up ... as a root out of dry ground." (Isaiah 53:2) Nazareth was considered to be an unfruitful place, dry ground. Philip said, "Come and see." Nathanael was a genuine seeker of truth, so he went with Philip to see Jesus.

When Jesus saw Nathanael, he said, "Behold an Israelite indeed, in whom is no guile." Jesus saw in Nathanael a true follower of God; in him was no deceit. Jesus' omniscience surprised Nathanael, and he asked, "How do you know me?" Jesus proved his divine power by telling Nathanael that he saw him under the fig tree before Philip called him. Only God could do that! Then Nathanael confessed to Jesus, "You are the Son of God; you are the King of Israel." If an unbeliever will honestly investigate Jesus, he will become a believer.

Jesus told his disciples that they would see greater proof of his divine nature. They would "see heaven open." Jesus would say, "I am the way, the truth, and the life; no man comes to the Father, but by me." (John 14:6) Jesus is the ladder that reaches up to heaven, like the one in Jacob's dream in Genesis 28:10-12. His kingdom would provide heavenly blessings.

The First Miraculous Sign of Jesus
John 2:1-11

Three days later, Jesus and his disciples attended a wedding in Cana of Galilee, which was the home of Nathanael (21:2). All the events from the questioning of John (1:19) to the wedding (2:1) occurred within one week. Jewish weddings included a feast in the bridegroom's home that lasted for several days. When they ran out of wine, Jesus' mother showed her faith in her son by informing him of this embarrassing situation. Jesus told her, "My hour is not yet come." His mission was not to provide for our physical needs. When he knew that he would soon die for our sins, Jesus said, "The hour is come, that the Son of Man should be glorified." (John 12:23-27) Mary said to the servants, "Whatever he says to you, do it." We all need to follow this good advice. Jesus told the servants to fill the six stone water pots with water. When they had completely filled them, he said, "Draw out." And when they did the water turned into wine, and it was better than the wine they had served before. This was the beginning of the miraculous signs of Jesus, and his disciples believed in him.

Jesus Goes to Capernaum
John 2:12

After the wedding in Cana, we do not know how much time elapsed before Jesus went to Capernaum with his mother, his brothers, and his disciples. Mary's home was in Nazareth, just four miles southeast of Cana. They probably were with Mary in Nazareth for about six months, because scholars believe the period of Jesus' ministry was three-and-a half years.

The Passover Feast in Jerusalem
John 2:13-25

When Jesus went to Jerusalem for the Passover, he found the temple was being desecrated by money changers and by those that were selling oxen, sheep, and doves. With a whip, he cleansed the temple, saying, "Take these things away; make not my Father's house a house of merchandise."

When the Jews asked him for a sign that he had the authority to do these things, Jesus answered, "Destroy this temple, and in three days I will raise it up." Jesus was speaking of his body being raised from the dead. His resurrection is the proof that he is the Christ, the divine Son of God. (Romans 1:3-4) At the beginning of his ministry, Jesus was speaking about his death and resurrection. This was his mission. He did not come to establish an earthly kingdom. The Jews misunderstood

Jesus. They thought he was talking about the temple that took forty-six years to build.

While Jesus was in Jerusalem for the Passover, he did miracles, which caused many to believe in him. Because Jesus knew what was in the hearts of men, he did not need to be told about any person.

Jesus Speaks of the New Birth to Nicodemus
John 3:1-21

Nicodemus, a Pharisee who was on the supreme court of the Jews, came to see Jesus while he was in Jerusalem. He addressed Jesus as "Rabbi," a respected teacher. He and others believed that God was with Jesus, because of the miracles that he did.

Jesus told Nicodemus that he must be born again in order to see the kingdom of God. Thinking Jesus was speaking of a physical birth, Nicodemus asked, "How can a man be born when he is old?" Jesus answered, "Unless one is born of water and the Spirit, he cannot enter the kingdom of God." NKJV Jesus is speaking of a spiritual new birth, that results in a change of life. As a teacher of Israel, Nicodemus should have known the promise of God in Ezekiel 36:26, "A new heart also I will give you, and a new spirit I will put within you." Jesus told Nicodemus that as Moses lifted up the serpent in the wilderness, even so the Christ must be lifted up on a cross to give eternal life to those who believe in him. "For God so loved the world, that he gave his only begotten Son, that whoever believes in him should not perish, but have everlasting life." (John 3:16) This is The Golden Text of the Bible. God sent his Son so that the world might be saved through him. Jesus is the light that has come into the world; but men love darkness rather than light, because their deeds are evil. He who loves the truth will come to the light of God.

The Final Testimony of John the Baptist
John 3:22-36

After his visit with Nicodemus, Jesus went into the Judean countryside to spend some time with his disciple; and they were baptizing those that were coming to Jesus. (4:2) At this time, John the Baptist was baptizing in Aenon near Salim, because much water was there. When it was reported to John that all were coming to Jesus, John said, "He must increase, but I must decrease. He that comes from above is above all." John ended his testimony by saying, "He that believes on the Son has everlasting life; and he that believes not the Son shall not see life, but the wrath of God abides on him."

Herod Puts John the Baptist in Prison
Luke 3:19-20; Matthew 4:12; John 4:1-3

John the Baptist had reproved Herod Antipas for marrying Herodias, his brother Philip's wife. So, Herod put John in prison. "When Jesus had heard that John was cast into prison, he departed into Galilee." Jesus knew that the Pharisees had heard that he made more disciples than John. This prompted him to go again into Galilee.

Jesus Goes Through Samaria
John 4:4

To travel from Judea into Galilee, the Jews normally would go around Samaria on the east side of the Jordan river; but it was the heavenly Father's will for Jesus to go through Samaria.

Jesus Teaches a Samaritan Woman
John 4:5-26

When Jesus came Jacob's well near the city of Sychar, he sat down on the well because he was weary. It was about noon, so his disciples went into the city to buy food. When a woman came to draw water, Jesus asked her for a drink. She replied, "How is it that you, being a Jew, ask a drink of me, who is a woman of Samaria?"

Jesus said, "If you knew the gift of God, and who it is that says to you, 'Give me to drink,' you would have asked of him; and he would have given you living water." Seeing that Jesus had nothing with which to draw water, she asked, "Are you greater than our father Jacob?" Jesus said, "Whoever drinks of this water shall thirst again; but whoever drinks of the water that I shall give him shall never thirst; but the water I shall give him shall be in him a well of water spring up into everlasting life."

The woman immediately said, "Sir, give me this water." Jesus said, "Go, call your husband, and come here." She replied, "I have no husband." Jesus said to her, "You have well said, 'I have no husband,' for you have had five husbands; and he whom you now have is not your husband. In that you said truly."

The woman said, "Sir, I perceive that you are a prophet." Not wanting to talk about her personal life, she asked Jesus about the place of worship. Is it Mount Gerizim or Jerusalem?

After saying that salvation is of the Jews, Jesus said, "The hour comes and now is, when the true worshipers shall worship the Father in spirit and in truth; for the Father seeks such to worship him." The geographical place does not matter; but the spiritual place does. Worship must be in spirit and in truth.

The woman said, "I know that Messiah comes, which is called Christ; when he is come, he will tell us all things." Jesus said to her, "I who speak unto you am he."

Many of the Samaritans Believe
John 4:27-44

At this time, his disciples came and were surprised to see Jesus talking with a Samaritan woman. In her excitement, she left her water pot and went into the city and said, "Come, see a man, who told me all things that I ever did. Is this not the Christ?" The Samaritans were expecting the coming of Christ. So, they went out to Jesus.

Meanwhile, Jesus was not interested in eating the food that his disciples brought to him. He explained, "My food is to do the will of him who sent me and to accomplish his work." ᴱˢⱽ As the people of Sychar dressed in white came to see him, Jesus said to his disciples, "Lift up your eyes and look on the fields; for they are white already to harvest."

Many of the Samaritans believed the testimony of the woman, and they begged Jesus to stay with them for two days. And then they said to the woman, "Now we believe, not because of your saying, for we have heard him ourselves and know that this is indeed the Christ, the Savior of the world." After two days at Sychar, Jesus departed to go into Galilee. The good reception that Jesus received in Samaria helps to explain the success of Philip the evangelist as he preached the gospel in Samaria years later. (Acts 8:5-17)

NOTES

The Early Ministry in Galilee

Jesus Comes into Galilee
Mark 1:14-15

Jesus came into Galilee, preaching the gospel of the kingdom of God. He preached, "The time is fulfilled, and the kingdom of God is at hand; repent and believe the gospel." Jesus came to fulfill the prophecy in Daniel 2:44 that in the days of the Roman kings, the God of heaven would set up a kingdom that would never be destroyed.

Jesus Heals a Nobleman's Son
John 4:45-54

The Galileans received Jesus, because they had seen his miracles during the Passover at Jerusalem. (John 2:23) Jesus came to Cana, where he had made the water wine. A nobleman who had a very sick son at Capernaum came to Jesus at Cana, requesting that he would come and heal his son, for he was at the point of death. But Jesus said, "Go your way; your son lives." And he was healed when Jesus said this. Jesus was in Cana, and the sick son was in Capernaum. Jesus could heal at a distance. This was the second miracle that Jesus did in Galilee.

Jesus Teaches in the Synagogue at Nazareth
Luke 4:14-30

When Jesus came to Nazareth, his hometown, he spoke in their synagogue and read the Scripture from Isaiah 61:1, "The Spirit of the Lord is upon me to preach the gospel to the poor; he has sent me to heal the brokenhearted, to preach deliverance to the captives, and recovering of sight to the blind, to set at liberty them that are bruised, to preach the acceptable year of the

Lord." And Jesus said to the people, "Today this Scripture is fulfilled in your ears."

The people said, "Is this not Joseph's son?" Jesus said, "No prophet is accepted in his own country." Then he gave the examples of Elijah and Elisha being rejected by their own people. Then those in the synagogue tried to kill him, but he went on his way.

Jesus Makes Capernaum His New Home
Matthew 4:13-17

Leaving Nazareth, Jesus went to Capernaum and made it his home. Jesus was preaching, "Repent, for the kingdom of heaven is at hand."

Jesus Calls His Disciples to be "Fishers of Men"
Matthew 4:18-22; Mark 1:16-20

When Jesus came to Capernaum, he walked by the Sea of Galilee and called four fishermen, Peter and Andrew, James and John, to follow him, promising that he would make them "fishers of men." They left their fishing nets and followed him into the city. Zebedee (the father of James and John) and the hired servants kept their fishing partnership going. (Mark 1:20)

Jesus in the Synagogue at Capernaum
Mark 1:21-28; Luke 4:31-37

When Jesus taught in the synagogue at Capernaum on the following Sabbath, the people were "astonished at his doctrine, for he taught them as one that had authority." A man was there with an unclean spirit, and the unclean spirit acknowledged Jesus as "the Holy One of God," who had the power to destroy them. When Jesus cast out the unclean spirit, the people were amazed and they said, "With authority he commands even the unclean spirits, and they obey him."

Jesus Heals Peter's Mother-in-Law
Mark 1:29-31; Luke 4:38-39; Matthew 8:14-15

When Jesus left the synagogue in Capernaum with Peter and Andrew, he entered their house with James and John. They found Peter's mother-in-law sick with a great fever, and Jesus healed her. Her complete recovery was instantaneous, because she immediately rose up and served them. Mark and Luke tell us when this miracle occurred. This story also proves that Peter was a married man.

Jesus Heals Various Diseases and Casts Out Demons
Matthew 8:16-17; Mark 1:32-34; Luke 4:40-41

Later that evening, those suffering with "various diseases" and those possessed with demons were brought to Jesus, and he healed "every one of them." Matthew places the healing of Peter's mother-in-law after the Sermon on the Mount along with other remarkable miracles in a topical arrangement of events to prove the great power of Jesus.

Jesus Preaches in Galilee
Mark 1:35-39; Luke 4:42-44; Matthew 4:23-25

After praying alone early the next morning, Jesus left Capernaum and began preaching in the synagogues throughout all Galilee, according to both Mark and Luke. Great crowds were coming to him, not only from Galilee but also from Judea and beyond the Jordan, according to Matthew.

Four Fishermen Forsake All to Follow Jesus
Luke 5:1-11

Jesus returned to the Sea of Galilee and found his four fishermen washing their nets. After preaching from Peter's boat, Jesus said to him: "Launch out into the deep and let down your nets for a catch." Peter was a professional fisherman, who knew that it was the wrong time of the day to fish. Although they had caught nothing after fishing all night, Peter said, "Nevertheless, at your word I will let down the net." And they caught so great a number of fish that their net was breaking. Peter then fell down at the feet of Jesus and said, "I am a sinful man." He had probably thought what Jesus had asked him to do was unless and foolish. This sign proved to him and to Andrew, James and John that by following Jesus they could "launch out into the deep" spiritually and become "fishers of men." Then "they forsook all and followed him." (Luke 5:11) Although they had been with Jesus in Galilee and Judea, they kept their fishing partnership, and they would fish from time to time.

Growing Popularity and Opposition

The Sermon on the Mount
Matthew 5 – 7

Great crowds of people were following Jesus from Galilee, Decapolis, Jerusalem, Judea, and from beyond the Jordan river. (Matthew 4:25) Seeing the multitudes, Jesus went up into a mountain; and his disciples came unto him. The traditional site for the Sermon on the Mount is a mountain located seven miles southwest of Capernaum called the Horns of Hattin, whose twin peaks form a natural amphitheater. In this sermon, Jesus explains the nature of the kingdom of heaven that was at hand. Multitudes had been following Jesus because he had been healing their sick. There was also talk that he could be the promised Messiah who would re-establish the kingdom of David. Jesus reveals the blessings in his kingdom would be spiritual, not physical.

The Beatitudes
Matthew 5:1-12

He began by saying, "Blessed are the poor in spirit, for theirs is the kingdom of heaven." Those that are humble before God will enter the heavenly kingdom of God. Those that have godly sorrow for their sins and that suffer hardships and trials will be comforted. The meek who practice self-control as they trust in the Lord will be truly blessed in this life and in the life to come. (cf. Psalm 37:11) The merciful will be given mercy; and those who hunger and thirst for righteousness will be filled. The pure in heart will see God; and God's children will be peacemakers. The kingdom of heaven is promised to those who are mistreated for doing right. Christ's disciples are to rejoice when they are persecuted for righteousness, because their reward in heaven is great.

Disciples Are to Be Salt and Light
Matthew 5:13-16

Jesus' disciples are to be the salt and light of the world. Salt purifies, preserves, and adds flavor. His disciples are not to be good for nothing; but they are to be the light of the world, like a city that is set on a hill. Jesus said, "Let your light so shine before men, that they may see your good works, and glorify your Father who is in heaven."

Jesus Fulfills the Law
Matthew 5:17-48

Jesus said, "Think not that I am come destroy the Law or the Prophets, I am not come to destroy but to fulfill." The law and the prophets prove that Jesus is the Christ. The law was "a shadow of good things to come." (Heb. 10:1) Jack P. Lewis offers this illustration: "As marriage does not nullify courtship but accomplishes its purposes, so the new system, while modifying, fulfills the law and the prophets." [20] Jesus calls for a righteousness that exceeds the righteousness of the scribes and Pharisees. Six times Jesus states what had been said, and then he adds, "But I say unto you." Jesus emphasizes the spirit behind the law; demanding more, not less. Jesus says, "Do not get angry," "Do not lust in your heart," "Do not divorce for just any reason," "Do not swear at all," "Do not resist an evil person," "Love your enemies."

Beware of Righteousness to be Seen of Men
Matthew 6:1-18

Jesus said, "Beware of practicing your righteousness before other people in order to be seen by them, for then you will have no reward from your Father who is in heaven." ESV Jesus mentions three acts that were commonly done to be seen by others: giving to the

---

[20] Jack P. Lewis, *The Gospel According to Matthew, Part I*, p. 86

needy, praying, and fasting. We are to do these things because of our devotion to God—not to be seen of men.

The Model Prayer
Matthew 6:9-15

We are to begin our prayer with reverence for God and end it with praise for his power and glory. We are to pray for God's will to be done as we ask for his physical and spiritual blessings. We are to forgive others as we pray for forgiveness.

How to Fast
Matthew 6:16-18

We should not fast (go without food) to be seen of men by looking deprived and unkept. Instead, we should care for our appearance and look normal when we fast. God knows when we fast, and he will reward us.

Treasures in Heaven
Matthew 6:19-24

Jesus tells us to lay up treasures in heaven where they will be secure. He gives another reason, "For where your treasure is, there will your heart be also." We need to see things clearly as they really are. We cannot serve two masters; we cannot serve God and material possessions.

Do Not Worry
Matthew 6:25-34

Jesus tells us not to worry about our life, what we will eat or what we will drink or what we will wear. Our Father in heaven feeds the birds and clothes the grass of the field. The birds of the air are free from anxiety as they search for the food God has provided. Our heavenly Father knows what we need. God may allow us to be hungry and to suffer need so we might learn to be content. (Phil. 4:11-12) Jesus promised, "But seek ye first the kingdom of God and his righteousness, and all these things shall be added unto you." Peter, Andrew,

James and John needed to hear this message of assurance, for they had just forsaken all to follow Jesus.

Judging Others
Matthew 7:1-6

Jesus condemns hypocritical faultfinding. We are not to judge others to make ourselves look good. We will be judged as we judge others. Jesus also says, "Give not that which is holy unto the dogs." Judgment is needed to discern those that are behaving like dogs. Jesus teaches in John 7:24, "Judge not according to appearance, but judge righteous judgment."

Keep Praying and Seeking the Truth
Matthew 7:7-12

"Ask, and it shall be given you; seek, and you shall find; knock, and it shall be opened unto you." Continued action is expressed in the Greek verbs: keep asking; keep seeking; keep knocking. You will receive good things from your heavenly Father, if you do not grow weary. If we keep seeking the truth, we will find it. The truth about how we are to treat others is summed up in the Golden Rule: "Therefore, all things whatsoever you would that men should do to you, do you even so to them."

Enter the Narrow Gate to Life
Matthew 7:13-14

The broad road leads to destruction, and there are many that are going that way. Jesus tells us to enter the narrow gate and travel the difficult way which leads to life, because there are few who find it."

Beware of False Prophets
Matthew 7:15-20

False prophets will come to us in sheep's clothing, but inwardly they are devouring wolves. Jesus says that we will know false teachers by their fruits.

Entrance into the Kingdom
Matthew 7:21-23

Calling Jesus "Lord" is not sufficient for entrance into the kingdom of heaven. One must be obedient to the heavenly Father's will. The kingdom of God is also called "the kingdom of heaven" to emphasize its spiritual and eternal nature. Many religious persons will be surprised on the day of judgment, when Jesus declares to them, "I never knew you. Depart from me, you who practice lawlessness."

The Wise and Foolish Builders
Matthew 7:24-27

Jesus compares a person who hears his teachings and obeys them to a wise man who built his house on the rock. The rain descended, the floods came, and the winds blew and beat on that house; and it did not fall, for it was founded on the rock. But everyone who hears Jesus but does not obey him is like a foolish man who built his house on the sand. And the rain descended, the floods came, and the winds blew and beat on that house; and it fell. And great was its fall.

The Response to the Sermon on the Mount
Matthew 7:28-29

"The crowds were amazed at his teaching, because he taught as one who had authority." NIV

Jesus Cleanses a Leper
Matthew 8:1-4, Mark 1:40-45, Luke 5:12-16

All three accounts relate this cleansing of a leper, because the wording is identical in all three. Matthew says that it occurred after the conclusion of the Sermon on the Mount, when Jesus had come down from the mountain. The man with leprosy believed that if Jesus was willing, he had the power to heal him. Jesus said, "I am willing." And immediately he healed him.

Jesus Forgives and Heals a Paralytic
Luke 5:17-26; Mark 2:1-12; Matthew 9:2-8

After some days, Jesus entered Capernaum again. While Jesus was preaching in a house, a paralytic carried by four men was brought to him, but they could not get to him because of the crowd. So, they uncovered the roof, and let down his bed. "When Jesus saw their faith," he said to the sick, "Son, your sins are forgiven you." Jesus proved he has the power to forgive sins by revealing the thoughts of those who were thinking he was blaspheming and by completely healing the man instantly.

Jesus Calls a Tax Collector to Follow Him
Matthew 9:9-13; Mark 2:13-17; Luke 5:27-32

The Jews despised the tax collectors, because they were working for the Roman government, and they often collected more taxes than what was due. Jesus conquered social prejudice by calling Matthew, a tax collector, to be his disciple. Mark and Luke use Matthew's other name, Levi. Luke tells us, "He left all" and followed Jesus. Matthew may have been one of the tax collectors that heard John the Baptist preach. (Luke 3:12-13) When criticized for eating with tax collectors and sinners, Jesus said he came to call sinners to repentance.

Jesus Attends the Passover in Jerusalem
John 5:1

Although John does not name this "feast of the Jews" in Jerusalem, it was probably the second Passover that Jesus attended during his ministry. This is the view of Irenaeus in the second century, and shared by the early church historian Eusebius in the third century, and many others since then. [21]

---

[21] B. W. Johnson, *The People's New Testament, Vol. I*, p. 342

Jesus Heals on the Sabbath
John 5:2-16

During this feast, Jesus healed a man on the Sabbath, which prompted Jesus to reveal his divine nature. The miracle took place at the pool of Bethesda in Jerusalem. A man who had been unable to walk for thirty-eight years was lying by the pool. Jesus healed him by simply saying, "Rise, take up your bed and walk." The man immediately got up and walked carrying his bed. But because it was on the Sabbath, the Jews told the man who had been healed, "It is not lawful for you to carry your bed." The man answered, "He that made me whole, said to me, 'Take up your bed and walk.'" Therefore, the Jews tried to kill Jesus because he had done these things on the Sabbath.

Jesus Claims His Divine Nature
John 5:17-30

Jesus then said, "My Father has been working until now, and I have been working." The Jews tried even more to kill him, because he was making himself equal with God. Jesus was God in the flesh. We all need to know Jesus as the Son of God. He said that the Father "has committed all judgment to the Son; that all men should honor the Son, even as they honor the Father. He that honors not the Son honors not the Father which has sent him ... Marvel not at this: for the hour is coming, in the which all that are in the graves shall hear his voice and shall come forth; they that have done good to the resurrection of life, and they that have done evil to resurrection of damnation."

Four Witnesses to Jesus
John 5:31-47

Jesus has four witnesses to prove his claims. **John the Baptist** testified that Jesus is the Son of God. (John 1:34) But an even greater witness were **the miracles** that Jesus did. Nicodemus had said to Jesus, "No man can do these miracles that you do except God is with him." (3:2) The third witness is **the Father** himself. When Jesus was baptized, a voice came from heaven, saying, "This is my beloved Son, in whom I am well pleased." The fourth witness is **the Scriptures** that testified of the coming of Christ. Jesus said, "Had ye believed Moses, ye would have believed me; for he wrote of me."

Many Women Minister to Jesus
Luke 8:1-3

Certain women who had been healed by Jesus went with him as he went through Galilee preaching; and they ministered to the needs of Jesus and his apostles out of their own resources. They are mentioned again as the first witnesses to Jesus' resurrection in Luke 23:55 – 24:10.

Jesus is Lord of the Sabbath
Luke 6:1-5; Matthew 12:1-8; Mark 2:23-28

Jesus and his disciples were going through the grain fields on the Sabbath, and the disciples plucked the heads of grain and ate, because they were hungry.

The Law permitted this; Deuteronomy 23:25 states, "When you come into your neighbor's standing grain, you may pluck the heads with your hands." However, the Pharisees criticized his disciples for working on the Sabbath—for reaping and preparing a meal on the day of rest. Jesus reminded them that David and his men were permitted to eat the holy bread when they were hungry. Also, the priests worked on the Sabbath day and were blameless. Jesus said, "If you had known what this means, 'I will have mercy, and not sacrifice,' you would not have condemned the guiltless." Jesus also stated, "The Sabbath was made for man, and not man for the Sabbath." The law did not require one to go hungry on the Sabbath. Jesus concluded, "Therefore the Son of man is Lord also of the Sabbath." He will do what is best for man.

Jesus Heals a Withered Hand on the Sabbath
Mark 3:1-6; Luke 6:6-11; Matthew 12:9-13

When Jesus entered the synagogue, there was a man with a withered hand. The Pharisees watched to see if he would heal on the Sabbath day, so they might accuse him. Jesus asked, "Is it lawful to do good on the Sabbath days?" Then when he had looked around on them with anger, being grieved for the hardness of their hearts, he said to the man, "Stretch forth your hand." And when he stretched out his hand. it was restored whole as the other. Jesus here gives us an example of righteous indignation, when he looked on the Pharisees with anger.

Jesus Is God's Chosen Servant
Matthew 12:14-21; Mark 3:6-12

After witnessing this great miracle, the Pharisees left the synagogue and plotted to kill Jesus. So, he withdrew from there; and great crowds followed him, and he healed them all. Jesus fulfilled the prophecy of Isaiah 42:1-4, "Behold my servant, whom I have chosen; my beloved, in whom my soul is well pleased. I will put my spirit upon him, and he shall show justice to the Gentiles".

NOTES

Jesus Instructs His Apostles

Jesus Chooses the Twelve Apostles
Mark 3:13-19; Luke 6:12-16

After spending the whole night in prayer on a mountain, Jesus called his disciples to him, and of them he chose twelve to be his apostles. This group would have greater power and authority to carry out his work of salvation than his other disciples. The twelve are listed also in Matthew 10:2-4 when Jesus sent them out on the limited commission. The names differ slightly in the lists because some of the apostles went by two names.

The Sermon on the Level Place
Luke 6:17-49

A large crowd was waiting for Jesus when he came down from the mountain and stood on a level place. After healing diseases and casting out demons, Jesus preached the Sermon on the Level Place. Those that are "poor" and "hunger now" are contrasted with those that are "rich" and "full." Jesus asked this important question in Luke 6:46: "Why call ye me, 'Lord, Lord,' and do not the things which I say?" Notice how this sermon differs from the Sermon on the Mount: (1) He came down from a mountain to preach on level ground; the one in Matthew was on a mountain. (2) He stood while he preached; he was seated when he gave the Sermon on the Mount. Although the sermons are similar, they are different.

Jesus Heals a Centurion's Servant
Luke 7:1-10; Matthew 8:5-15

After appointing the twelve apostles and preaching the Sermon on the Level Place, Jesus returned to

Capernaum and healed a centurion's servant. Matthew says the servant was paralyzed and suffering greatly; Luke says he was at the point of death. Matthew says that the centurion came to Jesus. Luke is more specific, saying that the centurion sent elders of the Jews to Jesus, requesting him to come and heal his sick servant. When Jesus and the elders came near to the house, the centurion sent friends to him, saying, "Lord, I am not worthy that you should come under my roof; but speak the word only, and my servant shall be healed. For I am a man under authority, having soldiers under me." This centurion who had one hundred soldiers under his authority recognized the authority and power of Jesus. "Speak the word, and my servant shall be healed." He believed that Jesus had power to heal at a distance. Jesus responded, "I have not found so great a faith, no, not in Israel." Only on two occasions, it is recorded that Jesus "marveled". He marveled here at the faith of a Roman centurion, and while in his hometown of Nazareth, "he marveled at their unbelief." (Mark 6:6)

Jesus Raises the Son of a Widow at Nain
Luke 7:11-17

The day after healing the centurion's servant at a distance, Jesus raised a man from the dead as he was being carried to his burial. The man was the only son of a widow, and Jesus "had compassion on her." Nain was six miles southeast of Nazareth.

John the Baptist Sends Messengers to Jesus
Luke 7:18-23; Matthew 11:1-6

When John was in prison, he heard about the works of Jesus. Luke says that he sent two of his disciples to the Lord, saying, "Are you he that should come? or look we for another?" In that very hour, Jesus healed many people. So, he answered them, "Go your way, and tell John what things you have seen and heard; how the blind see, the lame walk, the lepers are cleansed, and the deaf hear, the dead are raised, and to the poor the gospel is preached."

Jesus Praises John the Baptist
Matthew 11:7-15; Luke 7:24-30

John was more than a prophet. John was the messenger who prepared the way for the Christ in fulfillment of the prophecies of Isaiah 40:3 and Malachi 3:1. Jesus said, "Among those that are born of women there has not risen a greater than John; not withstanding he that is least in the kingdom of heaven is greater than he. ... And if you will receive it, he is Elijah, who was to come." John the Baptist fulfilled the prophecy in Malachi 4:5.

Woe to the Impenitent Cities
Luke 7:31-35; Matthew 11:16-24

Both John the Baptist and Jesus had been rejected by the majority of the Jews. Bethsaida, Capernaum, and other cities failed to repent, although Jesus had done his mighty works in them. It will be more tolerable for Tyre, Sidon, and Sodom on the Judgment Day than for these cities, because they would have repented if they had seen these mighty works.

Jesus' Prayer
Matthew 11:25-27

At that time, Jesus gave thanks to the Father for revealing the things of the gospel to his humble disciples, though the "wise" Jewish leaders did not understand them. Jesus repeats this prayer, after the seventy return from their mission work in Judea and beyond the Jordan River. (See Luke 10:1-24.)

The Great Invitation
Matthew 11:28-30

"Come unto me, all ye that labor and are heavy laden, and I will give you rest. Take my yoke upon you, and learn of me; for I am meek and lowly in heart; and ye shall find rest unto your souls. For my yoke is easy, and my burden is light."

Jesus Forgives A Sinful Woman
Luke 7:36-50

Jesus was eating with a Pharisee, when a sinful woman came in and stood at his feet weeping. (The Jews ate in a reclining position with their feet farthest away from the food.) The woman began washing his feet with her tears and drying them with the hair of her head. She kissed his feet and anointed them with precious ointment. The Pharisee thought to himself, "If this man were a prophet, he would know who is touching him and what kind of woman she is — that she is a sinner." NIV But Jesus showed him that he had the power to know what he was thinking. Jesus told this man, whose name was Simon, a parable about two debtors that were forgiven by the same creditor. One had owed ten times more than the other. Then Jesus asked Simon, "Which of them will love him most?" He answered, "I suppose that he to whom he forgave the most." Jesus said, "You have rightly judged." Then turning to the woman, Jesus asked, "Do you see this woman?" Reminding him of all that he had failed to do and all that she had done, Jesus concluded, "Wherefore I say unto you, her sins, which are many, are forgiven, for she has loved much; but to whom little is forgiven, the same loves little." Jesus said to the woman, "Your faith has saved you; go in peace."

The Crowds Prevented Jesus from Eating
Mark 3:20-21

The multitude crowded around Jesus, so that Jesus and his disciples could not eat. And his family begin seeking him to care for him, saying, "He has lost his senses." NASB

Jesus Is Accused of Casting Out Demons by Satan
Mark 3:22-27; Matthew 12:22-29; Luke 11:14-23

"The crowd brought to him a demon-possessed man who was blind and mute, and Jesus healed him, so that he could both talk and see. All the people were astonished and said, 'Is not this the Son of David?'" But the Pharisees accused Jesus of casting out demons by the prince of the demons. Jesus said, "Every kingdom divided against itself is brought to desolation ... If Satan cast out Satan, he is divided against himself; how then shall his kingdom stand? ... But if I cast out demons by the Spirit of God, then the kingdom of God is come unto you."

Sinning Against the Holy Spirit
Matthew 12:30-32; Mark 3:28-30

Jesus said, "He that is not with me is against me ... All manner of sin and blasphemy shall be forgiven unto men, but the blasphemy against the Holy Spirit shall not be forgiven." Jesus said this because they said, "He has an unclean spirit."

A Tree Is Known by Its Fruits
Matthew 12:33-37

Either make the tree good, and the fruit of it good; or else make the tree corrupt and the fruit of it corrupt. For out of the abundance of the heart the mouth speaks. A good man out of the good treasure of the heart brings forth good things; and an evil man out of the evil treasure brings forth evil things. For by your words you will be justified, and by your words you will be condemned.

The Sign of the Prophet Jonah
Matthew 12:38-42; Luke 11:29-32

Jesus would prove his deity by his resurrection from the dead. Jesus said. "For as Jonah was three days and three nights in the belly of the great fish, so will the Son of Man be three days and three nights in the heart of the earth." The men of Nineveh repented at (literally, *into*) the preaching of Jonah, and a greater than Jonah is here. Solomon was known for his great wisdom, and a greater than Solomon is here. The Christ is here!

Replace Evil with Good
Matthew 12:43-45; Luke 11:24-28

If we do not replace evil with good after being cleansed of our sins, our last condition will be worse than our first.

Jesus' Mother and Brothers
Matthew 12:46-50; Mark 3:20-21, 3:31-35; Luke 8:19-21

When his mother and brothers came looking for him, Jesus said, "Whoever shall do the will of my Father, who is in heaven, the same is my brother, and my sister, and mother."

The Parable of the Sower
Matthew 13:1-25; Mark 4:1-25; Luke 8:4-18

Matthew says it was the same day that his mother and brothers came looking for him, that Jesus taught this parable from a boat on the Sea of Galilee with the crowds on the shore. "The seed is the word of God." (Luke 8:11) As seed has life and power, so God's word is living and powerful. Different responses to the word are represented by four kinds of soils. The word of God is able to bless only those who will "keep it and bear fruit with patience" (Luke 8:15). Jesus said, "Take heed **how** you hear" (Luke 8:18) and "Take heed **what** you hear" (Mark 4:24). Only those who are seeking the truth will know the mysteries of the kingdom of heaven. (Luke 8:9-10) That is why Jesus spoke in parables.

The Parable of the Tares
Matthew 13:24-30, 36-43

The kingdom of heaven is compared to a farmer who sowed good wheat seed in a field, but his enemy sowed tares among the wheat during the night. The field is the world. Christ is the farmer. The good seed is God's word. The devil is the enemy who sows false teachings. The children of God are the wheat; the tares are Satan's children. The harvest is the judgment day. The reapers are God's angels, who will separate the good from the evil. And the righteous will have glory in heaven.

The Parable of the Mustard Seed
Matthew 13:31-32, Mark 4:30-32

The mustard seed is extremely small, but the plant grows quickly to be over ten feet tall. The kingdom of heaven would have a small beginning, but it would grow into a kingdom that would cover the earth, in fulfillment of Daniel 2:31-45.

The Parable of the Leaven
Matthew 13:33

The great influence that the kingdom of heaven would have in the world is compared to yeast that is added to bread dough.

Jesus Ended His Parables to the Multitude
Matthew 13:34-43

Jesus spoke these parables in fulfillment of Psalm 78:2. Then Jesus sent the multitude away and went into a house, where he explained the parables to his apostles and told them additional parables.

The Parable of the Hidden Treasure
Matthew 13:44

We should value the kingdom of heaven as a treasure worth sacrificing all that we have for it.

The Parable of the Costly Pearl
Matthew 13:45-46

We should be seeking the kingdom of heaven as our first priority in life, as this merchant was searching for a costly pearl.

The Parable of the Dragnet
Matthew 13:47-50

Jesus told his apostles that they would be "fishers of men." Like the dragnet in the sea, the kingdom would draw in people of various motives and characters, but there will be a separation of the unfaithful from the faithful at the end of time.

The Parable of a Lamp
Mark 4:21-23

All things will be revealed and come to light. Jesus said, "For there is nothing hid, which shall not be manifested; neither was anything kept secret, but that it should come abroad. If anyone has ears to hear, let him hear."

The Parable of Seedtime and Harvest
Mark 4:26-29

God gives life, growth, and harvest. Although man does not understand how this is possible, he plants the seed, cultivates the plant, and reaps the crop. (1 Cor. 3:6) This all takes time. God promised Abraham, "In your seed, all the nations of the earth shall be blessed." (Genesis 22:18) It took centuries for the kingdom of God to come into fruition, but with the coming of Christ, harvest time has come.

Jesus Instructs His Apostles
Mark 4:33-34; Matthew 13:51-52

After explaining the parables to the twelve, he asked them, "Have you understood all these things?" They answered, "Yes."

The Cost of Being His Disciple
Matthew 8:18-22

When Jesus saw the great crowds, he ordered his disciples to depart to the other side of the Sea of Galilee. As they were leaving a scribe came to Jesus and said, "Teacher, I will follow you wherever you go." Jesus answered, "Foxes have holes and birds of the air have nests, but the Son of Man has nowhere to lay his head." Someone else said to Jesus, "Lord, let me first go and bury my father." Jesus said to him, "Follow Me, but let the dead bury their own dead." NKJV His father may have not yet died, but the man wanted to delay following Jesus until after his father's death.

NOTES

The Great Power of Jesus

Jesus Calms the Storm at Sea
Mark 4:35-41; Luke 8:22-25 Matthew 8:23-27

Mark says that this miracle was "on the same day" that Jesus taught the parable of the sower. When evening had come, Jesus and his apostles crossed over the Sea of Galilee to the other side in the boat from which he had been teaching. A great storm suddenly arose while they were on the sea, but Jesus calmed the wind and the sea by simply saying, "Peace, be still!" This great miracle proved that Jesus was no mere man. At first his disciples were afraid of the storm, but after Jesus conquered it, they feared exceedingly and said to one another, "What manner of man is this, that even the wind and the sea obey him?" In this miracle, Jesus showed his power over the forces of nature. Luke also relates this calming of the sea after Jesus taught parable of the sower. Matthew includes it along with other miraculous signs to show the great power of Jesus.

Jesus Casts Out Demons
Matthew 8:28-34; Mark 5:1-21; Luke 8:26-39

This miracle took place on the eastern shores of the Sea of Galilee, in the country of the Gerasenes; Gerasa was one of the ten cities of Decapolis. Matthew mentions two demon-possessed men, but the one described by Mark and Luke probably was "the fiercer and the more notorious of the two." [22] The demon-possessed man had lost his own identity, because when Jesus asked him his name, a demon answer, "My name is Legion, for we are many." Legion knew Jesus was "the Son of the Most High God." After Jesus had cast out demons, the man was clothed and in his right mind.

---

[22] J. W. McGarvey, *Matthew and Mark*, p. 289

When the people saw this, they were afraid to be in his presence, and they asked Jesus to leave. This miracle proved the power of Jesus over supernatural forces. The restored man proclaimed what Jesus had done for him throughout Decapolis, a district dominated by ten associated Greek cities.[23] When Jesus crossed back over the Sea of Galilee, many people came to him.

Why Jesus' Disciples Were Not Fasting
Mark 2:18-22; Luke 5:33-39; Matthew 9:14-17

Jesus said that the friends of the bridegroom do not mourn while the bridegroom is with them. But they will fast when the bridegroom is taken away from them. The church fasted after the ascension of Jesus. (Acts 13:2-3) Also, the new covenant of Christ would not be the same as the old covenant of Moses. To mix the two covenants would be disastrous.

A Synagogue Ruler Seeks the Power of Jesus
Matthew 9:18-19; Mark 5:21-24; Luke 8:40-42

Matthew reports, "While he spoke these things unto them, behold, there came a certain ruler and worshiped him, saying, 'My daughter is even now dead; but come and lay your hand upon her, and she shall live.' And Jesus arose and followed him." Mark states, "Now when Jesus had crossed over again by boat to the other side, a great multitude gathered to Him; and He was by the sea. And behold, one of the rulers of the synagogue came, Jairus by name." NKJV Both Mark and Luke tell us that his name was Jairus and that his daughter was twelve years old. Luke adds that she was his only daughter. A great multitude followed Jesus to the house.

A Woman Is Healed of a Hemorrhage
Luke 8:43-48; Mark 5:25-34; Matthew 9:20-22

As Jesus was on his way with Jairus, a woman suffering from a hemorrhage sought to be healed by just

---
[23] F. N. Peloubet, *Peloubet's Bible Dictionary*, p. 145

touching the hem of his garment, and she was healed immediately. Jesus did in a moment what physicians could not do twelve years.

Jesus Raises the Daughter of Jairus from the Dead
Matthew 9:23-26; Mark 5:35-43; Luke 8:49-56

Before Jesus and Jairus arrived at the house, a messenger came, saying that his daughter was dead. Mourners had already gathered and were weeping. Jesus brought the dead girl back to life with just three words, "Little girl, arise." Then he ordered that she be given something to eat; this proved that she had been completely restored. Peter, James, and John were the only apostles that witnessed this great miracle that caused the fame of Jesus to spread abroad into all that land.

Jesus Heals Two Blind Men
Matthew 9:27-31

When Jesus departed from there, two blind men followed him, crying out and saying, "Son of David, have mercy on us!" They were acknowledging Jesus as the Messiah, the Christ. Jesus asked them, "Do you believe I am able to do this?" And they answered, "Yes, Lord." Then he touched their eyes, saying, "According to your faith be it unto you." And their eyes were opened. NKJV They could see. And when they had departed, they told everyone what Jesus had done for them. The signs and miracles of Jesus should make all men see that he is the Messiah, the King.

A Mute Man Speaks
Matthew 9:32-34

"As they went out," a man possessed with a demon was brought to Jesus because he could not speak. Demons afflicted people in many ways: blindness (Matthew 12:22), convulsions (Mark 1:26), deafness (Mark 9:25), crippled and bent over (Luke 13:11), and insanity. (Mark 5:15) When Jesus casted the demon out of the mute man, he was able to speak, and the crowds marveled. This miracle showed the power of Jesus over Satan.

Jesus Is Rejected at Nazareth Again
Mark 6:1-6; Matthew 13:53-58

After Jesus performed these miracles, Jesus "went out from there and came into his own country." The rejection of Jesus at Nazareth described in Luke came at the beginning of his Galilean ministry. The accounts in Matthew and Mark seem to be at a much later time. In Luke 4:22, his hometown people asked, "Is this not Joseph's son?" It appears that Joseph may have died before this visit recorded in Matthew and Mark; for here the people asked, "Is this not the Carpenter, the son of Mary?" There is no reference to Joseph. There are other differences in Luke's account and that of Matthew and Mark. The people reacted to the teaching of Jesus by attempting to kill him in Luke 4:28-29. At that time, they must have thought he was a blasphemer. In Matthew and Mark's accounts, the people were "astonished" at his wisdom, and they had heard of his "mighty works." But they "were offended" because he was one of them; he was "the brother of James, and Joses, Judas, and Simon." Jesus said, "A prophet is not without honor except in his own country, among his own relatives, and in his own house." Even his brothers did not believe in him. (John 7:5) Jesus marveled at their unbelief.

The Compassion of Jesus
Mark 6:6; Matthew 9:35-38

After being rejected again at his hometown of Nazareth, "Jesus went about all the cities and villages, teaching in their synagogues, and preaching the gospel of the kingdom, and healing every sickness and every disease among the people. But when he saw the multitudes, he was moved with compassion on them because they fainted and were scattered abroad, as sheep having no shepherd. Then he said to his disciples, 'The harvest truly is plenteous, but the laborers are few. Pray therefore the Lord of harvest, that he will send forth laborers into his harvest.'"

Jesus Sends Out His Twelve Apostles
Mark 6:7-13; Matthew 10:1 – 11:1; Luke 9:1-6

Mark says that Jesus sent them out "two by two". All the writers mention that Jesus gave them power to cast out unclean spirits and to heal the sick, but Matthew adds that they could cleanse the lepers and even raise the dead. In Matthew 10:10, Jesus explains why they should take very little with them, saying, "for the worker is worthy of his food." NKJV All accounts include instructions to "shake off the dust from your feet" when departing from those who would not hear their message. The apostles were not to go to the Gentiles or Samaritans; this commission was limited to "the lost sheep of the house of Israel." And they were to preach, "The kingdom of heaven is at hand."

Matthew's account is lengthier and includes many great teachings of Jesus. "Be ye therefore wise as serpents and harmless as doves." (10:16) "And you shall be hated of all men for my name's sake; but he that endures to the end shall be saved." (10:22) "It is enough for the disciple to be as his master, and the servant as his lord." (10:25) Jesus had just been rejected by his own people at Nazareth. "Fear not them which kill the body, but are not able to kill the soul." (10:28) "Whoever therefore shall confess me before men, him will confess also before my Father who is in heaven. But whoever shall deny me before men, him will I also deny before my Father who is in heaven." (10: 32-33) "Think not that I am come to send peace on earth; I came not to send peace, but a sword." (10:34) "He that loves father or mother more than me is not worthy of me." (10:37) "He that takes not his cross ... is not worthy of me." (v. 38) "He that receives you receives me; and he that receives me receives him that sent me." (Matthew 10:40)

When Jesus had finished instructing his apostles, he departed from there to teach and preach in the cities of Galilee. Jesus set the example. And the twelve apostles went out and preached that men should repent.

Herod Beheads John the Baptist
Luke 9:7-9; Mark 6:14-29; Matthew 14:1-12

When King Herod heard the report about Jesus and all that he did, he was perplexed and said, "John I have beheaded, but who is this?" And he desired to see Jesus. (Luke 9:7-9) Herod became convinced that Jesus was John the Baptist raised from the dead. Both Mark and Matthew relate the events leading to John's death. Herod had put John in prison because John had rebuked him for marrying Herodias, the wife of his brother. Luke mentioned this earlier in Luke 3:19-20. Herodias wanted to kill John, but Herod refused to do it because he feared John, knowing that he was a just and holy man. (Mark 6:19-20) Herod was so pleased when the daughter of Herodias danced before him on his birthday, he promised that he would give her whatever she wanted. Herodias told her to ask for the head of John the Baptist.

Jesus Feeds the Five Thousand
Matthew 14:13-21; Mark 6:30-44;
Luke 9:10-17; John 6:1-14

This is the only miracle found in all four gospels. Matthew says it was soon after the beheading of John the Baptist. Mark and Luke mention that the apostles had just returned from their mission work in Galilee. John says that the Passover feast was at hand. (John 6:4) Jesus and his apostles went by boat to a deserted place to get away from the people, but a great multitude had seen them leave and ran along the shore to meet them when they landed. Jesus was "moved with compassion" and began teaching them about the kingdom of God and healing those in need. Because it was getting late in the day, Jesus fed the multitude by multiplying five loaves and two small fish. Besides the women and children, about 5,000 men were fed with the bread and fish. There was plenty of food for everyone, because they took up twelve baskets full of the left-overs.

Jesus Walks on the Stormy Sea
John 6:15-21; Matthew 14:22-36; Mark 6:45-56

After feeding the 5,000, Jesus urged his disciples to get into the boat and go before him to the other side, while he went up on the mountain alone to pray. John 6:15 reveals that Jesus knew that people were about take him by force to make him king. In the night, a strong wind was blowing against the disciples' boat. Just before dawn, Jesus came walking on the sea. At first the disciples were afraid, thinking he was a ghost, but he said, "Be of good cheer, it is I, be not afraid." Peter's walking on the water and being rescued by Jesus is reported by Matthew, and he adds that when they got in the boat, the wind ceased, and the disciples worshiped Jesus, saying, "Of a truth you are the Son of God." They finally realized that Jesus is more than another David; he is deity. John adds that after Jesus and Peter got into the boat, immediately they were at the land where they were going. They landed at Gennesaret, and many were healed by touching the hem of his garment as he went on his way to Capernaum.

Jesus Is the Bread of Life
John 6:22-71

The following day, when the people realized that Jesus was not at the place where he had fed them, they got into boats and came to Capernaum, seeking him. Jesus said they sought him, not because they saw his miraculous signs, but because they ate the bread and were filled. He told them not to labor for food which perishes, but for that food which endures into everlasting life. Jesus would give this food to them, because God the Father had put his seal of approval upon him. When they asked him what they should do, Jesus replied, "This is the work of God, that you believe on him whom God has sent."

Wanting more free food, they asked Jesus for a sign, reminding him that Moses gave their fathers "bread from heaven." Jesus said, "The bread of God is he who comes down from heaven, and gives life unto the world." When they asked for this bread, Jesus said, "**I am the bread of life**; he that comes to me shall never hunger." Then Jesus declared, "I came down from heaven, not to do my own will, but the will of him that sent me … And this is the will of him that sent me, that everyone who sees the Son and believes on him may have everlasting life; and I will raise him up at the last day."

The Jews then complained because he said, "I am the bread of life which came down from heaven." They asked, "Is not this Jesus, the son of Joseph?"

Jesus then stated, "No man can come to me, except the Father who has sent me draw him; and I will raise him up at the last day. It is written in the prophets, 'And they shall be all taught of God.' Every man therefore that has heard and has learned of the Father comes unto me."

And Jesus concluded, "It is the Spirit who gives life; the flesh profits nothing. The words that I speak to you are spirit, and they are life." NKJV

After hearing this message, many of his disciples left him and ceased following him. Then Jesus said to his apostles, "Will ye also go away?" Peter answered, "Lord, to whom shall we go? You have the words of eternal life." Then Jesus said that one of the twelve was a devil, referring to Judas Iscariot.

NOTES

The Year of Opposition

The Passover was at hand when Jesus fed the 5,000 and walked on the sea. A year later, Jesus would be put to death at the next Passover. "Jesus went around in Galilee, purposely staying away from Judea because the Jews there were waiting to take his life." ᴺᴵⱽ (John 7:1) Beginning the last year of his ministry, he went to Phoenicia, Decapolis, Caesarea Philippi, and Perea to escape the threats of the Jews and to have more time to be alone with his apostles.

Jesus Condemns the Commandments of Men
Mark 7:1-13; Matthew 15:1-9

Some scribes and Pharisees came to Galilee from Jerusalem to find fault with Jesus. They criticized him for allowing his disciples to eat with unwashed hands. This violated the tradition of the elders. Jesus said Isaiah had prophesied of their hypocrisy when he wrote: "This people draw nigh unto me with their mouth, and honor me with their lips, but their heart is far from me. But in vain they do worship me, teaching for doctrines the commandments of men." The Pharisees had rejected the commandments of God in order to keep their own traditions.

Defilement Comes from Within
Matthew 15:10-20; Mark 7:14-23

Jesus said, "Not that which goes into the mouth defiles a man; but that which comes out of the mouth, this defiles a man." When Jesus had said these things, his disciples told him that the Pharisees were offended. Jesus did not apologize, but he said, "Every plant which my heavenly Father has not planted shall be rooted up." Then he concluded, "For out of the heart proceed evil thoughts, murders, adulteries, fornications, thefts, false witness, blasphemies. These are the things which defile a man." Mark adds to the list of those things that defile: covetousness, wickedness, deceit, lasciviousness, an evil eye, pride, and foolishness. (7:22)

A Gentile Shows Her Faith in Jesus
Mark 7:24-30; Matthew 15:21-28

Jesus and his disciples went to Phoenicia, the region of Tyre and Sidon, looking for a quiet retreat. However, a woman who had a demon-possessed daughter came to Jesus for help. Matthew calls her "a woman of Canaan," indicating she was a Gentile of Palestine. Mark says she was "a Greek, born in Syrian Phoenicia." ^{NIV} A Greek ruler, Antiochus IV whose capital city was Antioch in Syria, desecrated the temple in Jerusalem in 168 BC. Now a Greek woman from that area came to Jesus begging him to cast the demon out of her daughter. Jesus first rejected her, saying that the children's bread should not be given to the dogs. She said, "Truth, Lord, yet the dogs eat of the crumbs which fall from the master's table." Jesus responded, "O woman, great is your faith; be it unto you even as you will." The woman believed Jesus would be using only a very small portion of his great power to heal her daughter. The gospel that was preached first to the Jews would be more widely accepted by the Gentiles.

Jesus Heals in Decapolis
Matthew 15:29-31; Mark 7:31-37

Jesus departed from the regions of Tyre and Sidon and went around the eastern shores of the Sea of Galilee into the region of Decapolis. Jesus healed a deaf man with a speech impediment. And the people were astonished, saying, "He has done all things well." Matthew adds that Jesus went upon a mountain near the sea; and he healed those that were lame, blind, mute, maimed, and many others. And the great multitudes gloried God.

Jesus Feeds the Four Thousand
Mark 8:1-10; Matthew 15:32-39

The multitudes had been with Jesus in for three days, and they had nothing more to eat. Jesus fed four thousand by multiplying seven loaves and a few small fish; and the leftovers filled seven large baskets.

The Sign Seekers Test Jesus
Matthew 15:39 – 16:4; Mark 8:10-12

After feeding the 4,000, Jesus got into a boat with his disciples and came to Dalmanutha, an area on the west side of the Sea of Galilee. They went to Magadan, also called Magdala, a town a few miles northwest of Tiberias. The Pharisees and Sadducees demanded of Jesus a sign from heaven. Jesus said, "There shall no sign be given unto this generation." And then referring to his resurrection from the dead he said, "There shall no sign be given unto it, but the sign of the prophet Jonah."

The Leaven of the Pharisees & Sadducees
Mark 8:13-21; Matthew 16:5-12

Jesus and his disciples got into a boat on the western shores of the Sea of Galilee and departed to the northern shores. As they sailed, Jesus said, "Beware of the leaven of the Pharisees and of the Sadducees." Mark says, "the leaven of the Pharisees and of Herod," because the Sadducees were closely associated with the Herodians, a political party. The disciples thought he said this because they had failed to bring enough bread. Jesus reminded them of his feeding both the five thousand and the four thousand. Then they understood that he was warning them of the teaching of the Pharisees and of the Sadducees. Leaven represents influence; the disciples were not to be influenced by them.

The Pharisees were hypocritical, and the Sadducees were political and worldly minded.

Jesus Heals a Blind Man at Bethsaida
Mark 8:22-26

Jesus and his disciples came ashore at Bethsaida, the home of Peter and Andrew. (John 1:44) Bethsaida was divided by the Jordan River as it flowed into the Sea of Galilee. The city on the east side of the river was called Bethsaida Julia; and the city on the west side, Bethsaida of Galilee. [24] Galilee was also called Gennesaret. The western part of the city was in the province of Galilee, and the eastern part was in Gaulanitis.[25] Capernaum was just a short distance west of Bethsaida; and the place where Jesus had fed the five thousand was southeast of the city. When Jesus came into Bethsaida, they brought a blind man to him to be healed. Jesus led the blind man out of the village, and he restored his sight in two stages. At first, men looked like trees walking about; and then he saw everything clearly.

Peter's Confession & Christ's Promise
Mark 8:27-30; Luke 9:18-20; Matthew 16:13-20

Leaving Bethsaida, Jesus and his disciples traveled to the region of Caesarea Philippi, a city twenty-five miles to the north. Jesus was seeking to have some time alone with his disciples, so he could reveal himself more fully to them. On the way, as Jesus was praying with them (Luke 9:18), he asked, "Whom do men say that I the Son of man am?" They answered, "Some say you are John the Baptist, some Elijah, and others Jeremiah or one of the prophets." Then Jesus said, "But who do you say that I am?" Peter answered, "You are the Christ, the Son of the living God." Then Jesus told Peter that his confession was not the opinion of men but the revelation of God. This confession would be the rock upon which

---

[24] F. N. Peloubet, *Peloubet's Bible Dictionary*, p. 91
[25] *The Westminster Historical Atlas to The Bible*, p. 80

Christ would build his church, and even death would not prevent it. Peter would be given the keys of the kingdom of heaven. He would open the doors of Christ's church on the day of Pentecost by preaching that Jesus is Lord and Christ and by telling those who believed in Jesus to "repent and be baptized ... in the name of Jesus Christ for the remission of sins." (Acts 2:38) "And the Lord added to the church daily such as should be saved." (Acts 2:47)

Jesus Predicts His Death and Resurrection
Matthew 16:21-23; Mark 8:31-33; Luke 9:21-22

Jesus began to tell his disciples that he "must go to Jerusalem and suffer many things ... and be killed, and after three days rise again." Peter objected, saying, "Lord, this shall not be unto you." Jesus rebuked Peter and told him that he was not being mindful of the things of God, but the things of men. Peter was like the blind man at Bethsaida when he was seeing men that looked like trees; Peter would not see clearly Christ and his mission until after Jesus' death, and resurrection, and ascension into heaven.

Jesus Describes Discipleship in His Kingdom
Luke 9:23-27; Mark 8:34 – 9:1; Matthew 16:24-28

Jesus explained to the crowd and to his disciples, what one must do to be his disciple. First, he must **deny himself** by surrendering his own way to Christ in repentance. Second, he must **take up his cross** daily in obedience to God, being willing to suffer for him. Third, he **must follow** the teachings and example of Jesus. A person will find life by losing his life in unselfish service in the kingdom, by putting Christ's interests above one's personal interests. Jesus asked, "What shall it profit a man, if he shall gain the whole world, and lose his own soul?" If we are ashamed of Christ, he will be ashamed of us when he comes in the glory of God and the holy angels. Jesus concluded, "There are some of them that stand here, which shall not taste of death, till they have seen the kingdom of God come with power." (Mark 9:1)

Jesus Is Transfigured on the Mount
Matthew 17:1-8; Luke 9:28-36; Mark 9:2-8

In the region of Caesarea Philippi, Jesus had just told his disciples of his approaching death and resurrection and of the coming of the kingdom of God. Matthew and Mark both say that "after six days" Jesus took Peter, James, and John up on "a high mountain." Caesarea Philippi was at the base of Hermon, a very high mountain. Luke reports that Jesus "went up on the mountain to pray." This is a clear reference to Mount Hermon. Luke says this event was "about eight days" later. The New International Versions translates eight days as "a week later" in John 20:16. Luke describes the time less specifically than Matthew and Mark. While on the mountain Jesus was transfigured in glory with Moses and Elijah to strengthen the faith of the three apostles. Luke reports that Moses and Elijah were talking with Jesus about his approaching death. Peter recalled this event in 2 Peter 1:16-18 to prove that "we have not followed cunningly devised fables, when we made known unto you the power and coming of our Lord Jesus Christ, but were eyewitnesses of his majesty."

Jesus Explains the Prophecy Concerning Elijah
Mark 9:9-13; Matthew 17:9-13

As they came down from the mountain, the apostles asked, "Why do the scribes say that Elijah must come first?" NKJV They were referring to Malachi 4:5-6. Jesus told them that Elijah had come, and they did not know him, but did to him whatever they wished. When he added that he also would suffer at their hands, they understood that he was speaking of John the Baptist.

Jesus Heals a Demon Possessed Boy
Matthew 17:14-21; Luke 9:37-42; Mark 9:14-29

When Jesus came down from the mountain the next day, he saw a great multitude around his disciples that had been left behind. The apostles had power to cast out demons (Mark 6:7); but they were unable to cast out a demon that was possessing a man's only son. The boy's father said to Jesus, "If you can do anything, have compassion upon us and help us." Jesus said, "If you can believe, all things are possible to him who believes." Jesus rebuked the demon, and it came out of him, and the child was cured from that very hour. This was an unusually difficult case. Jesus emphasized to his disciples the importance of their faith. The only way they could have cast out the demon was by prayer and fasting. Immediately after his being transfigured in glorious majesty, Jesus demonstrated his great power over Satan.

Jesus Again Predicts His Death and Resurrection
Mark 9:30-32; Luke 9:43-45; Matthew 17:22-23

They departed from there and passed through Galilee. Jesus did not want anyone to know where they were, because he was teaching his disciples about himself and his mission. He said to them, "The Son of Man is to be betrayed into the hands of men. They will kill him, and after three days he will rise." ^{NIV} But his disciples did not understand him and were afraid to ask. Matthew adds, "And they were exceedingly sorrowful."

The Temple Tax Is Paid
Matthew 17:24-27

When Jesus and his disciples were come to Capernaum, the officials that collected the half-shekel temple tax came to Peter and asked him, "Doesn't your teacher pay the temple tax?" "Yes, he does," he replied. ^{NIV} This tax was not compulsory but voluntary. Although Jesus is the Son of God for whose house the tax was being collected, Jesus paid the tax. He instructed Peter to catch a fish; and when he opened the fish's mouth, he would find a shekel with which to pay the tax for him and Peter.

The Feast of Tabernacles at Hand
John 7:2-9

The Feast of the Tabernacles was approaching; this feast lasted eight days in late September and early October. It was a time of thanksgiving for the fruitful harvest and a remembrance of God's care for the Israelites during their time in the wilderness. After this feast, only six months remained in the earthly ministry of Jesus, for he would be crucified during the next Passover.

The brothers of Jesus were sarcastically encouraging him to go to the feast, because they did not believe in him at this time. Jesus refused to go with them. He wanted to go through Samaria.

After the resurrection of Jesus, his brothers, the sons of Joseph and Mary, believed in him. (Acts 1:14) James and Jude were among the writers of the New Testament.

Jesus Goes through Samaria to Jerusalem
John 7:10, Luke 9:51-56

Jesus did not travel openly with the other Jews who went on the east side of the Jordan River on their way to the feast, but he and his disciples went through Samaria secretly. Luke says that "the time was come for him to be received up," that is to suffer death, to be resurrected, and to ascend into heaven. Knowing this, Jesus "steadfastly set his face to go to Jerusalem." He knew that this was his mission, and he was determined to fulfill it. Since he was going to die for all, he would travel through the land of the Samaritans. An unnamed village in Samaria would not receive Jesus because he was on his way to Jerusalem. James and John asked

Jesus if they should send down fire from heaven and consume them, but he turned and rebuked them. Some Greek manuscripts add that Jesus said, "You do not know what manner of spirit you are of. For the Son of man is not come to destroy men's lives, but to save them." They went on to a more receptive village.

The Cost of Discipleship
Luke 9:57-62, Matthew 8:19-22

As they went on the road to Jerusalem, someone said to Jesus, "Lord, I will follow you wherever you go." A scribe had made the same statement earlier as Jesus was getting into a boat in Matthew 8:19-22. They both received the same response from Jesus, "The foxes have holes and birds of the air have nests, but the Son of man has not where to lay his head." Jesus may have said this to everyone who desired to be his disciple. Another man wanted to bury his father before following Jesus. These are examples of the cost of discipleship, even though they may have been at different times and places. Luke adds another example. On the road to Jerusalem, another said he would follow Jesus, but he first desired to go home and bid his family farewell. Jesus said, "No one, having put his hand to the plow, and looking back, is fit for the kingdom of God."

The Seventy Are Sent Out
Luke 10:1-16

Jesus appointed seventy disciples to go before him in Judea and beyond the Jordan to prepare the way. They were to heal the sick and preach the good news of the kingdom of God. He sent them out two by two. Two witnesses would add credibility to their message, and they would encourage each other. He was training them to be evangelists after his return to heaven. The instructions were similar to those given to the twelve apostles before their mission in Galilee. However, the seventy differed from the apostles in that their appointment was only temporary. Jesus repeats the woes upon the impenitent cities of Chorazin, Bethsaida, and Capernaum. There were seventy in the Sanhedrin, just as there were seventy elders that assisted Moses. (Numbers 11:16-17, 25)

The Ministry in Judea

The Feast of Tabernacles
John 7:11-13

The hostile Jewish leaders were seeking Jesus at the feast. The people were discussing Jesus. Some said, "He is a good man;" and others said, "No; he deceives the people." But they did this quietly for fear of the Jews.

Jesus Teaches in the Temple
John 7:14-24

Halfway through the feast, Jesus went into the temple and taught the people. He said, "My doctrine is not mine, but his that sent me. If any man will do his will, he shall know the doctrine, whether it be of God or whether I speak of myself." Jesus compared his healing on the Sabbath with the Jews performing circumcision on the Sabbath, in order that the law would not be broken. Jesus taught, "Judge not according to appearance, but judge righteous judgment." (v. 24)

The People Notice Jesus' Boldness
John 7:25-36

The Jews sought to take Jesus; "but no man laid hands on him, because his hour was not yet come." Many of the people believed on Jesus as the Christ, being impressed by his miracles. Therefore, officers were sent to arrest Jesus.

Jesus Offers the Living Water
John 7:37-39

The last day of the Feast of Tabernacles was a special day. A priest filled a golden pitcher with water from the pool of Siloam and led the people to the temple, repeating these words from Isaiah 12:3, "With joy you will draw water from the wells of salvation."

Then the priest poured out the water onto the altar, which was a symbol of the pouring out of the Holy Spirit. [26] Moses brought water from a Rock in the wilderness on two occasions. (Exodus 17:1-5; Numbers 20:2-11) That spiritual Rock that gave water to the people represented Christ. (1 Cor. 10:4) Jesus cried out to those at the feast, "If anyone is thirsty, let him come to me and drink. Whoever believes in me, as the Scripture has said, streams of living water will flow from within him." [NIV] (Isaiah 44:3) Jesus was speaking of the Spirit; for the Holy Spirit was not yet given, because Jesus had not yet died and ascended to heaven.

The Response of the People
John 7:40-44

Many of them said, "Of a truth this is the Prophet." (Deut. 18:15-18) Others said, "This is the Christ." But some said, "Shall the Christ come out of Galilee?" They did not know that Jesus was born in Bethlehem, Judah. There was division among them.

The Response of the Authorities
John 7:45-53

The officers that had been sent to arrest Jesus returned to the Jewish rulers without him. When asked why, the officers said, "No one ever spoke like this man." The Jews then asked, "Have any of the rulers or the Pharisees believed on him?" Nicodemus, who was one of the rulers, spoke up and asked, "Does our law judge any man, before it hears him?" He was a believer!

A Woman Caught in Adultery
John 8:1-11

The next day, the scribes and Pharisees brought to Jesus a woman caught in adultery. After reminding Jesus

---

[26] Frank Pack, *The Gospel According to John, Part I*, p, 130

that the law said an adulterer should be stoned, they asked him what he would say. They were tempting him, so they might be able to accuse him of breaking the law. The fact that they did not also bring the man to be stoned for his adultery revealed their hypocrisy; they were not interested in obeying the law. Leviticus 20:10 states, "The adulterer and the adulteress shall be put to death." Jesus did not answer them, but he stooped down and wrote with his finger in the dust. We don't know what he wrote; but it could have been this Scripture. Jesus then stood up and said, "He that is without sin among you, let him first cast a stone at her." And he stooped down again and continued writing. Starting with the eldest they went out one by one, being convicted by their own conscience. When Jesus stood up, he saw only the woman; and he said to her, "Neither do I condemn you; go, and sin no more." God wants all sinners to come to repentance. (Read 2 Peter 3:9.)

Jesus is the Light of the World
John 8:12-20

Jesus said, "I am the light of the world; he that follows me shall not walk in darkness, but have the light of life." When the Pharisees accused him of bearing his own witness, Jesus said, "It is also written in your law, that the testimony of two men is true. I am one that bears witness of myself, and my Father who sent me bears witness of me." Jesus spoke these words as he taught in the temple.

The Identity of Jesus
John 8:21-30

Jesus said he was going away; and where he was going, the Pharisees could not come, because they would die in their sins. Jesus stated, "I am not of this world. I said therefore to you, that you shall die in your sins; for if you believe not that I am …, you shall die in your sins." The word *"he"* is in *italics* because it has been added by the translators. Jesus is claiming to be the "I AM" – the eternal God of Exodus 3:14. He said, "When you have lifted up the Son of Man, then you shall know that I AM … The Father has not left me alone; for I always do those things that please him." Many believed Jesus when he said this.

Jesus Promises Freedom from Sin
John 8:31-38

Then Jesus said to those Jews who believed in him, "If you continue in my word, then you are my disciples indeed; and you shall know the truth, and the truth shall make you free." The Jews who did not believe in Jesus protested, and asked him, "How do you say, 'You shall be made free?'" Jesus replied, "Whoever commits sin is the slave of sin. If the Son therefore shall make you free, you shall be free indeed."

The True Children of God
John 8:39-45

The unbelieving Jews said Abraham was their father. Jesus said, "If you were Abraham's children, you would be doing the works Abraham did, but now you seek to kill me, a man who has told you the truth that I heard from God. This is not what Abraham did. You are doing the works your father did." Then the Jews said, "We have one Father—even God." Jesus said, "If God were your Father, you would love me; for I came from God and I am here. I came not of my own accord, but he sent me." And then Jesus said, "You are of your father the devil, and your will is to do your father's desires. He was a murderer from the beginning, and has nothing to do with the truth, because there is no truth in him. When he lies, he speaks out of his own character, for he is a liar, and the father of lies." ᴱˢⱽ True children of God will do what God desires them to do.

Jesus Claims His Eternal Existence
John 8:46-59

Jesus asked the unbelieving Jews, "Which of you convicts me of sin? And if I say the truth, why do you not believe me?" The Jews then accused Jesus of being a Samaritan and having a demon. Jesus said if anyone would keep his word, he would never see death. They asked him, "Are you greater than Abraham?" Jesus said, "Your father Abraham rejoiced to see my day; and he saw it and was glad." Although Abraham had died physically, he was still alive; he knew when Jesus came to this world to save us. Then Jesus said to them, "Before Abraham was, I AM."

Jesus Heals a Man Born Blind
John 9:1-41

Jesus said that a man was born blind so "that the works of God should be made manifest in him." And he added, "I must work the works of him that sent me while it is day; the night comes when no man can work."

Jesus spat on the ground and made clay, and anointed the blind man's eyes with the clay. Then he instructed the blind man to wash in the pool of Siloam; and when he did, he came back seeing.

This man was brought before the Pharisees. Some of them said that Jesus was not of God, because he had healed the blind man on the Sabbath day. Others rhetorically asked, "How can a man that is a sinner do such miracles?" There was division. The man who had been healed stated, "Since the world began it has been unheard of that anyone opened the eyes of one who was born blind." NKJV He told the Pharisees, "If this man were not from God, he could do nothing." And the Pharisees cast him out of the synagogue.

Then the man with sight confessed his faith in Jesus and worshiped him. And Jesus said, "For judgment I am come into this world, so that the blind will see; and those that see will become blind." ᴺᴵⱽ Saul of Tarsus, a Pharisee, was made blind so he could see the truth. (Acts 9:8)

Jesus Is the Good Shepherd
John 10:1-21

Jesus said, "I am come that they might have life, and that they might have it more abundantly. I am the good shepherd; the good shepherd gives his life for the sheep." Speaking of those of other nations, Jesus said, "Other sheep I have, which are not of this fold; them also I must bring, and they shall hear my voice. And there shall be one fold and one shepherd." Jesus said he had power lay down his life and to take it again. When some accused Jesus of having a demon, others said, "Can a demon open the eyes of the blind?"

The Seventy Return with Joy
Luke 10:17-20

When the seventy returned, Jesus told them not to rejoice because the demons were subject to them, but to rejoice that their names were written in heaven.

Jesus Gives Thanks to the Father and Rejoices
Luke 10:21-24

Jesus gives thanks to the Father for revealing his great power to the seventy during their successful mission. In Matthew 11:25-27, Jesus prayed the same prayer on a different occasion.

The Parable of the Good Samaritan
Luke 10:25-37

After quoting the law, "You shall love your neighbor as yourself," a lawyer tried to justify himself by asking Jesus, "And who is my neighbor?" Jesus answered with the parable of the Good Samaritan. We should be a neighbor to anyone in need, even to those who may have prejudices against us.

Jesus in the Home of Martha
Luke 10:38-42

As Jesus and his disciples went through Judea, they came to the village of Bethany; and Martha invited him into her home. As she was busy preparing a meal for him, her sister Mary sat at Jesus' feet and listened to his teachings. Martha complained that Mary had left her to do all the work. Jesus said, "Martha, Martha, you are careful and troubled about many things; but one thing is needful; and Mary has chosen that good part, which shall not be taken away from her."

Jesus Teaches His Disciples to Pray
Luke 11:1-4

When one of his disciples requested that he teach them to pray, Jesus gave them a model prayer that is similar to the one he had given in the Sermon on the Mount in Matthew 6:9-13.

The Parable of a Friend at Midnight
Luke 11:5-13

If you have a friend who will get up from his bed at midnight to help you in a time of need, surely God will answer your prayer if you keep praying persistently. Jesus said, "Ask, and it shall be given you; seek, and ye shall find; knock, and it shall be opened unto you." Jesus had taught this same lesson earlier in his Sermon on the Mount. There are some truths that are worthy repeating.

Jesus Eats with a Pharisee
Luke 11:33-54

A Pharisee asked Jesus to eat with him. Using this as an opportunity to teach an important lesson about inner purity, Jesus deliberately failed to wash his hands before eating. Jesus said, "You Pharisees make the outside of the cup and dish clean, but your inward part is full of greed and wickedness." ^{NKJV} One of the lawyers said to Jesus, "You reproach us also." Jesus replied, "Woe to you also, lawyers! For you load men with burdens hard to bear, and you yourselves do not touch the burdens with one of your fingers." ^{NKJV} Jesus concluded, "You have taken away the key of knowledge; you entered not in yourselves, and them that were entering in you hindered." Jesus would later repeat these teachings and "woes" to the scribes and Pharisees during his last week, as recorded in Matthew 23.

Warnings and Encouragements
Luke 12:1-12

Jesus is teaching lessons to his followers in Judea that he had previously taught privately to his apostles in Galilee. He said, "Beware of the leaven of the Pharisees, which is hypocrisy." "Be not afraid of them that kill the body." We must confess Jesus before others.

The Parable of the Rich Fool
Luke 12:13-21

This parable was prompted by one in the crowd who asked Jesus to make his brother divide the inheritance with him. Jesus warned, "Beware of covetousness; for a man's life consists not in the abundance of the things which he possesses." Jesus illustrated this truth with the parable of the rich man whose land produced abundant crops. While planning to build greater barns and anticipating a life of ease, God said to him, "You fool, this night your soul shall be required of you; then whose shall those things be which you have provided?" Jesus concluded, "So is he that lays up treasure for himself, and is not rich toward God."

Do Not Worry
Luke 12:22-34

The rich man was preoccupied with the things of this world. Jesus tells his disciples not to worry about earthly things, but rather to seek the kingdom of heaven. He had already taught about God's caring for our earthly needs in the Sermon on the Mount. On this occasion, Jesus adds, "Fear not, little flock, for it is your Father's good pleasure to give you the kingdom."

Be Watchful for the Master's Return
Luke 12:35-48

"Be ye therefore ready also, for the Son of man comes at an hour when you think not." "And that servant, which knew his lord's will and prepared not himself, neither did according to his will, shall be beaten with many stripes. But he that knew not, and did commit things worthy of stripes, shall be beaten with few stripes."

Jesus Came to Send a Fire
Luke 12:49-53

Jesus said, "I am come to send fire on the earth." Anthony Ash says that the *fire* most likely refers to "the coming of the Holy Spirit and the spread of the gospel." [27] Fire is a symbol of judgment. Jesus asks, "Do you suppose that I came to give peace on earth? I tell you, not at all, but rather division." NKJV His truth separates those that accept it from those that reject it. The peace promised by the angels at his birth is the inner peace of God in the mind and heart of the believers. [28]

Discern the Times
Luke 12:54-59

The people could discern the clouds and winds and know the weather that would come, but they could not

---

[27] Antony Lee Ash, *The Gospel According to Luke, Part II*, p. 46
[28] **Luke 2:13-14, John 14:27, John 16:33**

discern the signs of the Christ and his approaching kingdom. The time to settle your wrongs is before coming to trial by the judge.

Repent or Perish
Luke 13:1-5

Some in the crowd told Jesus of the Galileans whose blood Pilate had mixed with their sacrifices at the temple. Jesus asked them, "Do you suppose that these Galileans were worse sinners than all other Galileans, because they suffered such things?" He said, "I tell you, no; but unless you repent you will all likewise perish." Jesus also reminded them of the eighteen people that were killed when the tower of Siloam fell on them. Such tragedies should serve as warnings to all that the Judgment Day is coming and that we should repent of our sins.

The Parable of the Barren Fig Tree
Luke 13:6-9

A man planted a fig tree, expecting fruit after the normal three years of maturity. When it continued to be fruitless, he ordered that it be cut down. The three-year period stands for the Jews' opportunity to repent during the ministry of Jesus. Jerusalem was destroyed in AD 70. This parable explains why Jesus cursed the fig tree during the last week before his death.

Jesus Heals a Crippled Woman on the Sabbath
Luke 13:10-21

As Jesus was teaching in a synagogue on the Sabbath, he saw a woman that had a spirit of infirmity for eighteen years and was bent over. He healed her, so immediately she was made straight. But the ruler of the synagogue criticized Jesus for healing her on the Sabbath. Jesus called him a hypocrite, because each of them would untie his ox or donkey on the Sabbath to give it water. Jesus asked, "And ought not this woman, being a daughter of Abraham, whom Satan has bound, lo, these eighteen years, be loosed from this bond on the Sabbath day?" His accusers were ashamed. Then Jesus again compared the kingdom of God to a grain of mustard seed and to leaven.

Jesus Goes to Jerusalem for Hanukkah
Luke 13:22; John 10:22-23

"And he went through the cities and villages, teaching, and journeying toward Jerusalem." ᴸᵘᵏᵉ "At that time the Feast of Dedication took place at Jerusalem; it was winter, and Jesus was walking in the temple in the portico of Solomon." ᴶᵒʰⁿ, ᴺᴬˢᴮ Hanukkah is the Hebrew word for dedication; and the Jews still celebrate this festival in December.

The Jews Confront Jesus
John 10:24-30

The Jews surrounded Jesus and demanded that he tell them plainly if was the Christ. They were seeking evidence to accuse Jesus of blasphemy. Jesus said he had told them; he often referred to himself as the "Son of Man," which was a term used by Daniel for the Christ. (Daniel 7:13-14) The miracles of Jesus bore witness that he was from God, whom he called his Father.

Jesus promises eternal life to those who hear his voice and follow him; and no one will be able pluck them out of his hand. Jesus said, "I and my Father are one." Jesus plainly told them that he was the Christ, the divine Son of God.

The Jews Attempt to Stone Jesus
John 10:31-38

The Jews took up stones to stone Jesus. He asked them, "Many good works have I shown you from my Father, for which of those works do you stone me?" He had casted out demons, healed the sick, and even raised the dead. They answered, "It is not for a good work that we are going to stone you but for blasphemy, because you, being man, make yourself God." ᴱˢⱽ Jesus indeed was God in the flesh. Jesus reminded them that Psalms 82 speaks of Israel's judges as "gods," because they were to judge according to God's law, and "the Scripture cannot be broken." If mere men were called "gods" because God gave his will to them, how much more so is it true of the one "whom the Father **sanctified** and sent into the world." Jesus is the Word of God, who became flesh to bring God's word to men. The word ***sanctified*** is a synonym for **dedicated**. Jesus was the "dedicated one" at the Feast of Dedication. The works of Jesus proved his claims.

The Ministry in Perea

Jesus Escapes to Perea
John 10:39-42

Jesus was able to escape from the Jews who were seeking to arrest him. And he went into Perea beyond the Jordan River to the place where John was baptizing at first. "And many people came to him. They said, "Though John never performed a miraculous sign, all that John said about this man was true. And in that place, many believed in Jesus." NIV

Jesus Teaches about Greatness
Mark 9:33-37; Luke 9:46-48; Matthew 18:1-4

Jesus returned to Galilee for a brief visit. When they came to Capernaum and were in the house, Jesus asked his apostles, "What were you discussing on the way?" ESV They remained silent, because they had been discussing who would be the greatest in the kingdom. This discussion may have been prompted by Jesus' promising the keys of the kingdom to Peter and by his allowing only Peter, James and John to go with him up on Mount Hermon. (Matthew 16:19; 17:1) Jesus said to them, "If any man desires to be first, the same shall be last of all, and servant of all." Jesus then set a little child in their midst and said, "Except you be converted, and become as little children, you shall not enter into the kingdom of heaven. Whoever therefore shall humble himself as this little child, the same shall be the greatest in the kingdom of heaven."

Those with Childlike Faith
Matthew 18:5-10

Jesus said, "Whoever shall receive one such little child in my name receives me." David Roper observes, "As the message progressed, the term 'little ones' was expanded to include not only children, but also disciples with a child-like faith." [29] If someone should cause such a one to sin, it would be better for him to be hanged or drowned. Woe to the man by whom offence comes. We should get rid of anything that causes us or others to sin. "Take heed that you despise not one of these little ones." Their angels are watching over them.

Forgiveness, Faith, and Duty
Luke 17:1-10

We should not cause a brother to fall away by our refusing to forgive him. Jesus said, "If your brother sins, rebuke him, and if he repents, forgive him. If he sins against you seven times in one day, and seven times comes back to you and says, 'I repent,' forgive him." When the apostles heard this, they said, "Increase our faith!"

Speaking of duty, Jesus taught, "You also, when you have done everything you were told to do, should say, 'We are unworthy servants; we have only done our duty.'" NIV We must guard against having pride in our good deeds. We cannot earn salvation; it is a gift from God. (Romans 6:23)

Concern for the Lost
Matthew 18:11-22

Jesus said, "For the Son of man is come to save that which was lost." If a man lost a sheep, he would leave ninety-nine sheep to find the lost one. "Even so, it is not the will of your Father which is in heaven that one of these little ones should perish." If your brother sins against you, tell him his fault in private, but if he will not hear you, take with you one or two witnesses. If he will not hear them, tell it to the church. But if he fails to repent, let him be disfellowshipped. "Whatever you

---

[29] David L. Roper, Truth for Today Commentary, *The Life of Christ*, 1, p. 572

bind on earth shall have been bound in heaven; and whatever you loose on earth shall have been loosed in heaven." ᴺᴬˢᴮ Our actions must be according to God's truth established in heaven. Jesus promises, "Where two or three are gathered together in my name, there am I in the midst of them." Then Peter asked the Lord, "How oft shall my brother sin against me, and I forgive him? Till seven times?" Jesus said to him, "I say not unto thee seven times; but, until seventy times seven."

The Parable of the Unforgiving Servant
Matthew 18:23-35

Jesus compared the kingdom of heaven to a king that had a servant who owed him "ten thousand talents." This was an enormous debt that he could not possibly pay. When the king commanded that the servant and his family be sold along with all that he had, the servant begged for mercy. Then the king was moved with compassion and forgave him the entire debt.

But that servant found one of his fellow servants who owed him a hundred denarii and demanded to be paid immediately. This was a significant amount of money, about a third of a laborer's yearly income; but his fellow servant could have paid the debt if given enough time. However, the forgiven servant took his fellow servant and threw him into prison until he should pay the entire debt. When the king was informed his actions, the king said to him, "O you wicked servant, I forgave you all that debt, because you desired me. Should you not also have compassion on your fellow servant, even as I had pity on you?" The king was angry and delivered the unforgiving servant to the torturers until he should pay all that was due him. Jesus concluded, "So likewise shall my heavenly Father do also unto you, if you from your hearts forgive not everyone his brother their trespasses."

Jesus Condemns a Sectarian Spirit
Mark 9:38-50; Luke 9:49-50

Upon hearing these teachings, John confessed, "We saw someone casting out demons in your name, and we tried to stop him, because he was not following us." But Jesus said, "Do not stop him, for no one who does a mighty work in my name will be able soon afterward to speak evil of me. For the one who is not against us is for us." ᴱˢⱽ This man must have been with Jesus in his teaching, because Jesus said in Matthew12:30, "He that is not with me is against me." Anyone who gives you a cup of cold water in the name of Christ, because you belong to him, will not lose his reward. Jesus said, "Have salt in yourselves, and have peace one with another." ᴹᵃʳᵏ

Jesus Leaves Galilee
Matthew 19:1-2; Mark 10:1

"When Jesus had finished these sayings, he departed from Galilee, and came into the coasts of Judea beyond the Jordan." Jesus came again to Perea on the east side of the Jordan River on his way to Jerusalem. He taught the great multitudes that followed him and healed their sick and afflicted.

Jesus Teaches about Marriage and Divorce
Matthew 19:2-9; Mark 10:2-9

The Pharisees came to Jesus testing him about divorce, saying, "Is it lawful to divorce one's wife for any cause?" ᴱˢⱽ Jesus reminded them of God's plan for marriage from the beginning. God ordained marriage to be between a man and a woman; and the two become one. Jesus concluded, "What therefore God has joined together, let not man put asunder." Jesus said that Moses had authorized "a bill of divorcement" (Deut. 24:1-4), because of the hardness of their hearts; but from the beginning it was not so. Jesus wants us to have a marriage like God ordained. Instead of looking for a reason to divorce; we should be seeking ways to strengthen our marriage. Jesus added, "Whoever shall put away his wife, except it be for fornication, and shall marry another, commits adultery; and whoever marries her which is put away commits adultery."

Jesus Teaches about Marriage and Celibacy
Mark 10:10-12; Matthew 19:10-12

When Jesus entered a house, his disciples asked him again about marriage. He plainly said, "Whoever divorces his wife and marries another commits adultery against her, and if she divorces her husband and marries another, she commits adultery." His disciples said to him, "If such is the case of a man with his wife, it is better not to marry." Jesus replied, "Not everyone can receive this saying, but only those to whom it is given. For there are eunuchs who have been so from birth; and there are eunuchs who have been made eunuchs by men; and there are eunuchs who have made themselves eunuchs for the kingdom of heaven. Let the one who is able to receive this receive it." ESV Not everyone can live a life of celibacy, according to Jesus. The Holy Spirit also teaches, "Because of the temptation to sexual immorality, each man should have his own wife, and each woman her own husband." ESV (1 Corinthians 7:2)

Jesus Blesses Little Children
Matthew 19:13-15; Mark 10:13-16; Luke 18:15-17

They brought little children and infants to Jesus that he might bless them. Jesus said, "Permit little children, and forbid them not, to come unto me; for of such is the kingdom of heaven."

A Rich Young Ruler Comes to Jesus
Mark 10:17-22;
Matthew 19:16-22; Luke 18:18-23

As Jesus was going out on the road, one came running and knelt before him. All the writers tell us that he was rich and that he asked Jesus, "What shall I do to inherit eternal life?" Matthew says he was **young**; Luke adds that he was a **ruler**. The rich man addressed Jesus as "Good Teacher" or "Good Master." And in Matthew he asked, "What **good** thing shall I do that I may have eternal life?" In all the accounts, Jesus tells him that only God is **good**. Jesus asked him, "Why do you call me good?" Did the young ruler recognize Jesus' divine nature? He had observed the ten commandments, but he asked Jesus, "What lack I yet?" Mark tells us that Jesus loved him. Jesus knew this likeable young man was trusting in his wealth. So, he told him to sell what he had and give to the poor and follow him so he could have treasure in heaven, but he went away sorrowful. Our good deeds cannot earn eternal life!

Jesus Teaches About True Riches
Mark 10:23-31;
Matthew 19:23-30; Luke 18:24-30

Jesus observed, "How hard it is for those who trust in riches to enter the kingdom of God." The kingdom of God does not promise material prosperity in our life on earth, so it is hard for the rich to value it. But Jesus added, "With God all things are possible." Peter said, "We have left all, and followed you." Jesus answered, "There is no man that has left house, or brothers, or sisters, or father, or mother, or wife, or children, or lands for my sake and the gospel's, but he shall receive a hundredfold now in this time, houses, and brothers, and sisters, and mothers, and children, and lands, with persecutions, and in the world to come eternal life."

The Few that Will Be Saved
Luke 13:23-30

Someone asked Jesus, "Lord, will those who are saved be few?" And he said, "Strive to enter through the narrow door. For many, I tell you, will seek to enter and will not be able." Jesus taught that when once the master of the house has shut the door, some will knock at the door, saying, "Lord, open to us," then he will answer them, "I do not know where you are from." Then they will say, "We ate and drank in your presence and you taught in our streets." But he will say, "I do not know where you come from. Depart from me, all you workers of evil!" ᴱˢⱽ Then there will be weeping and gnashing of teeth when they see Abraham and Isaac and Jacob and all the prophets along with people from the east and west in the kingdom of God, but they are cast out. Barclay writes, "When this questioner asked his question, he would certainly do so on the assumption that the Kingdom of God was for the Jews only, and that the Gentiles would all be shut out. Jesus' answer must have come as a shock to him. Jesus declared that the entry to the Kingdom can never be automatic, and that it is the result and reward of a struggle. 'Keep on striving to enter,' said Jesus." [30] We must deny ourself, take up our cross and follow Jesus. (Luke 9:23)

Herod's Threat to Kill Jesus
Luke 13:31-33

Pharisees came to Jesus with this warning: "Get out and depart from here for Herod will kill you." This had to be a false plot. Herod refused to condemn Jesus to death, when given the opportunity in Luke 23:6-11. It has been suggested that Herod wanted Jesus out of his territory of Perea, but he did not want to kill him. So, he made up this false plot and sent the Pharisees to Jesus advising him to leave. This is why Jesus said to them, "Tell that fox, 'Behold, I cast out demons, and I do cures today and tomorrow, and the third day I shall be perfected.'" Jesus called him a "fox" – a sly, cunning person. He let Herod know that he was not afraid of him. He must finish his work and eventually go to Jerusalem to die.

---

[30] William Barclay, *The Gospel of Luke*, p. 188

Jesus Laments over Jerusalem
Luke 13:34-35

"O Jerusalem, Jerusalem, which kills the prophets, and stones them that are sent unto thee; how often would I have gathered your children together, as a hen gathers her brood under her wings, and you would not. Behold your house is left desolate." This lament is repeated again in Matthew 23:37-39, on the Tuesday before his death.

Jesus at a Pharisee's House
Luke 14:1-6

One of the rulers of the Pharisees invited Jesus to his house to eat on the Sabbath. Other invited guests included a man with dropsy. They were watching Jesus closely to see what he would do. Jesus asked the lawyers and Pharisees, "Is it lawful to heal on the Sabbath?" If they answered, "Yes", they would have violated their tradition; if they answered, "No", they would have denied mercy. So, they kept silent. Jesus healed the man. Then he reminded them if their donkey or ox fell into a pit, they would immediately pull him out on the Sabbath.

The Exaltation of the Lowly
Luke 14:7-14

When Jesus noticed how the guests chose the best places, he told a parable that showed the wisdom of taking the lowest place when invited to a banquet. "For whoever exalts himself shall be abased; and he that humbles himself shall be exalted." Then Jesus said to his host, "When you give a banquet, invite the poor, the crippled, the lame, the blind, and you will be repaid at the resurrection of the righteous." NIV

The Parable of the Great Supper
Luke 14:15-24

The kingdom of heaven is like a certain man who prepared a great supper. The Jewish leaders were those that were invited, but they made excuses for not going. So, the poor and disabled among the Jews were invited; and they came. However, there was still room. Those from the highways, the Gentiles, were the last to be invited; and they also came.

Leaving All to Follow Christ
Luke 14:25-33

Jesus said, "If anyone comes to me, and does not hate his father and mother and wife and children and brothers and sisters, yes, and even his own life, he cannot be my disciple." ᴱˢⱽ The word **hate**, as used here by Jesus, means **to love less**. Jacob loved Rachel more than he loved Leah in Genesis 29:30; and in the next verse, the Lord saw that Leah was **hated**. We need to count the cost of being Christ's disciple. Jesus must come first. We are to love him more than any other person or thing.

Tasteless Salt is Worthless
Luke 14:34-35

Jesus taught, "Salt is good, but if it loses its saltiness, how can it be made salty again? It is fit neither for the soil nor for the manure pile; it is thrown out." ᴺᴵⱽ The disciples of Jesus are to be salt in the world. Similar words are in the Sermon on the Mount in Matthew 5:13-16. Jesus concluded, "He that has ears to hear, let him hear."

Jesus Is Criticized for Receiving Sinners
Luke 15:1-2

The Pharisees and scribes criticized Jesus for associating with the tax collectors and sinners who came to hear him. He responded by telling three parables.

The Parable of the Lost Sheep
Luke 15:3-7

If any of Jesus' critics lost one of his sheep, he would search for it until he found it; and he would rejoice with his friends. Jesus concluded, "Likewise joy shall be in heaven over one sinner that repents."

The Parable of the Lost Coin
Luke 15:8-10

If a woman with ten pieces of silver loses one coin, she will seek diligently for it. And when she finds it, she will rejoice with her neighbors. Jesus said that there is joy in the presence of God's angels over one sinner that repents."

The Parable of the Lost Son
Luke 15:11-32

Jesus compares a sinner to a young man who left home with his inheritance and wasted it with sinful living in a far country. When he had spent it all, he got a job feeding hogs. He became hungry and then realized that life would be better being a servant in his father's house. He made up his mind to return to his father and confess his sins. He would say, "I am no more worthy to be called your son; make me one of your hired servants."

When the father saw his son coming at a great distance, he had compassion on him; and he ran to him and hugged and kissed him. The wasteful son said, "Father, I have sinned against heaven, and I am no more worthy to be called your son." But his father interrupted his confession. He said, "Bring forth the best robe and put it on him; and put a ring on his finger and shoes of his feet." He ordered a celebration feast. He said, "For this my son was dead, and is alive again; he was lost and is found." Jesus is asking the Pharisees, if the lost sinner were your own penitent son, would you welcome him?

But the Pharisees were acting like the older brother in the rest of the story. He was angry that his brother had returned, and they were celebrating. He would not join the celebration. So, his father went out to him. In his self-righteousness, he told his father, "I have served you these many years and never at any time transgressed your commandment, but you never gave me such a party." He seems envious of his younger brother. He will not call him his brother, but he said, "As soon as this your son was come, who has devoured your money with harlots, you have killed for him the fatted calf." This older son also was lost; he did not value the blessing of living in his father's house. So, the father said to him, "Son, you are ever with me, and all that I have is yours. It was right that we should make merry, and be glad; for this **your brother** was dead, and is alive again; and was lost, and is found."

The father in the story represents God, our heavenly father. Do we appreciate the blessings of being with him? Do we rejoice when a sinner repents and returns home?

The Parable of the Dishonest Steward
Luke 16:1-14

The dishonest steward used money to accomplish his goals. We are to make proper use of money by helping the needy and evangelizing the world that we may have true riches in heaven. Jesus said, "He that is faithful in that which is least is faithful also in much; he that is unjust in the least is unjust also in much." We cannot serve God and material wealth. We are to be good stewards of God's blessings. Pharisees sneered at him when they heard this parable and his teachings, because they were covetous—they loved money.

God Knows Our Hearts
Luke 16:15-18

Jesus said to the Pharisees, "You are they which justify yourselves before men; but God knows your hearts. For that which is highly esteemed among men is abomination in the sight of God." They were more concerned about being "highly esteemed among men" than obeying God's law. The following story illustrates these lessons.

The Rich Man and Lazarus
Luke 16:19-31

The rich man was esteemed as a success as he lived a life of luxury. Poor Lazarus seemed to be a failure as he sat by the rich man's gate, longing for the scraps from his table and being noticed only by the dogs that licked his sores. Lazarus died, and the angels carried him to the side of Abraham. The rich man also died. He likely had an elaborate funeral; but in hades, he was in torment. He could see Abraham far away with Lazarus by his side. Abraham told the rich man to remember how he failed to help Lazarus, and now Lazarus could not help him, because there was a great chasm that could not be crossed between the two places. Then the rich man asked Abraham to send Lazarus back to warn his five brothers. However, Abraham said, "If they will not hear Moses and the prophets, neither will they be convinced though one rose from the dead."

Whether historical or a parable, the story teaches these seven great truths: (1) The soul of a man lives on after death; (2) The soul is still conscious and can remember life on earth; (3) The righteous go to a place of comfort and peace, but the wicked to a place of torment and misery; (4) The selfish use of wealth will bring suffering beyond the grave; (5) There is no changing of eternal destiny after death; (6) God's word is sufficient to save us; (7) The rich man was not guilty of doing wrong things, but he sinned by failing to do the right things.

Some try to dismiss the teachings of this story by saying that it is a parable. But remember—all of the parables that Jesus told were true to life experiences.

NOTES

Jesus Returns to Bethany

Jesus Raises Lazarus from the Dead
John 11:1-46

While teaching on the east side of the Jordan River, Jesus received a message from Bethany, the town of Mary and her sister Martha, whose brother Lazarus was sick. Jesus loved this family. When Jesus heard that Lazarus was sick, he said, "This sickness is not unto death, but for the glory of God, that the Son of God might be glorified thereby." Jesus stayed in Perea for two more days.

Then he said, "Let's go into Judea again." His disciples reminded him that the Jews were attempting to kill him. Jesus said, "Our friend Lazarus sleeps, but I go, that I may awake him." His disciples said, "If he sleeps, he shall do well." Then Jesus told them plainly, "Lazarus is dead. And I am glad for your sakes that I was not there, to the intent you may believe; nevertheless, let us go unto him." Then Thomas said, "Let us also go, that we may die with him."

When Jesus came to Bethany, he found that Lazarus had been in the grave four days. Bethany was less than two miles from Jerusalem; and many of the Jews came from the city to comfort Martha and Mary. As soon as Martha heard that Jesus was coming, she went out to meet him. She said to Jesus, "Lord, if you had been here, my brother would not have died. But I know, that even now, whatever you will ask of God, God will give it you." Jesus said, "Your brother shall rise again." Martha had been listening to Jesus, and so she said, "I know that he shall rise again in the resurrection at the last day." (John 6:40)

Jesus said to her, "I am the resurrection and the life; he that believes in me, though he were dead, yet he shall live; and whoever lives and believes in me shall never die. Do you believe this?" She said, "Yes, Lord. I believe that you are the Christ, the Son of God, who should come into the world."

Then Martha went and secretly called her sister Mary, saying, "The Master has come, and he calls for you." Mary came to Jesus to where he was outside of the town, and the Jews followed her thinking she was going to the grave. Mary expressed her confidence that if Jesus had been there, her brother would not have died. Jesus groaned in his spirit when he saw her and the others weeping. He asked, "Where have you laid him?" And they said, "Lord, come and see." **Jesus wept.** As the song says, "Jesus cares, I know He cares; His heart is touched with my grief." Then the Jews said, "Behold, how he loved him."

When they came to the grave, which was a cave, covered with a stone, Jesus said, "Take away the stone." Martha said, "Lord, by this time he stinks; for he has been dead four days." Jesus said to her, "Did I not say to you that if you would believe, you would see the glory of God?" NKJV Then they took away the stone, and Jesus lifted up his eyes toward heaven and prayed, "Father, I thank you that you have heard me. And I know that you hear me always; but because of the people which stand by I said it, that they may believe that you have sent me." Then he cried out with a loud voice, **"Lazarus come forth."** And he that was dead came forth bound with graveclothes. Jesus said to them, "Loose him, and let him go."

Many of the Jews that had seen these things believed in Jesus. But others went to the Pharisees and told them what Jesus had done.

The Plot to Kill Jesus
John 11:47-53

The Sanhedrin had an emergency meeting. This council of the Jews was composed of both Pharisees and Sadducees. Many witnesses had seen Jesus bring Lazarus back to life, a man who had been dead for four days! They could not deny this great miracle; but these Jewish leaders still would not believe in Jesus as the divine Son of God.

They were not interested in the truth; their only concern was keeping their positions of power. Caiaphas, the high priest said, "It is expedient for us, that one man should die for the people, and that the whole nation perish not." As high priest, God inspired him to prophesy that "Jesus would die for that nation; and not for that nation only." The Jewish leaders plotted to put Jesus to death, because he had raised Lazarus from the dead. All these things were according to "the determined purpose and foreknowledge of God." (Acts 2:23)

Jesus Retreats to Ephraim
John 11:54

Jesus was aware of the plot to kill him, so he did not walk openly among the Jews. He withdrew to the village of Ephraim, which was northeast of Jerusalem and near the wilderness of Judea on the westside of the Jordan River and close to the border of Samaria. This was a relatively unpopulated area.

NOTES

The Journey for the Passover
Luke 17:11

As the Passover was approaching, Jesus went from Ephraim northward through Samaria into Galilee. There he joined the Galileans who were going on the eastside of the Jordan through Perea to Jerusalem for the Passover.

Jesus Cleanses Ten Lepers
Luke 17:11-19

When ten lepers cried out to Jesus to have mercy on them, he told them to go and show themselves to the priests. As they went by faith, they were cleansed. But only one came back to thank him, and he was a Samaritan. Jesus asked, "Were there not ten cleansed? But where are the nine?"

The Nature of the Kingdom of God
Luke 17:20-21

When the Pharisees asked Jesus when the kingdom of God would come, he said, "The kingdom of God does not come with your careful observation, nor will people say, 'Here it is,' or 'There it is,' because the kingdom of God is within you." ᴺᴵⱽ It would not be on a map, because it is a spiritual kingdom.

Christ's Second Coming
Luke 17:22-37

Jesus told his disciples not to be deceived by false Christs that would come. When Jesus returns, it will be like lightning which lights up the sky from one end to the other. His coming would be unexpected as the flood in the days of Noah and as the fire that rained down from heaven and destroyed everyone in Sodom. Jesus said, "Remember Lot's wife."

The Parable of the Persistent Widow
Luke 18:1-8

The purpose of this parable is revealed in verse one: "Then Jesus spoke a parable to them, that men always ought to pray and not lose heart." ^{NKJV} The delay in Jesus' coming again should not discourage us; we should keep praying. A widow seeking justice came before a corrupt judge who did not fear God nor regard man. He would not act for a while, but later he did avenge her, because he was getting weary of her continual coming to him. Jesus asked, "And shall not God avenge his own elect, which cry day and night unto him, though he bears long with them?"

The Parable of the Pharisee and the Tax Collector
Luke 18:9-14

"And he spoke this parable unto some who trusted in themselves that they were righteous, and despised others." A Pharisee and a tax collector went up to the temple to pray. The Pharisee thanked God that he was not like other men, and he reminded God of his fasting and giving. But the tax collector bowed his head and beat his breast, saying, "God, be merciful to me a sinner." Jesus said, "This man went down to his house justified rather than the other: for everyone that exalts himself shall be abased; and he that humbles himself shall be exalted."

Jesus Predicts His Death and Resurrection
Luke 18:31-34; Mark 10:32-34; Matthew 20:17-19

Jesus said, "Behold we go to Jerusalem, and all things that are written by the prophets concerning the Son of man shall be accomplished." This time he predicts that he would be mocked and scourged before his crucifixion and his resurrection.

The Servant is the Greatest
Matthew 20:20-28;
Mark 10:35-45

Matthew says that James and John came with their mother to Jesus, requesting the right to sit one on his right hand and the other on his left in his kingdom. When the other apostles heard it, they were greatly displeased. But Jesus said that his kingdom would not be like those of the nations, where the rulers and the great ones lorded over others with authority. He explained, "Whoever desires to be first among you, let him be your slave—just as the Son of Man did not come to be served, but to serve, and to give His life a ransom for many." NKJV

Jesus Heals Blind Bartimaeus
Mark 10:46-52;
Matthew 20:29-43; Luke 18:35-43

Jesus was traveling with a great multitude on the way to the Passover; this would be his last journey to Jerusalem. Matthew says that two men were healed, but only one is mentioned by Mark and Luke. It could be that Bartimaeus was the more outspoken of the two, or that he was well-known in the early church. He was a blind beggar that believed Jesus could restore his sight. He cried out to Jesus, addressing him as "the Son of David"—the Messiah. This miracle took place as they left the old Jericho inhabited by the poorer Jews (Matthew, Mark) and as they came near to the new Jericho, which was built by the Herod kings (Luke). This new city contained the palace and houses of the wealthy.[31] The story of Zacchaeus took place in the new Jericho.

---

[31] Homer A. Kent, Jr., *The Wycliffe Bible Commentary*, Matthew, p. 965

Jesus and Zacchaeus
Luke 19:1-10

Jesus was passing through the new Jericho, where the wealthy lived. Zacchaeus, the rich chief tax collector, wanted to see Jesus, but he was short of stature. So, he ran ahead of the crowd and climbed up into a sycamore fig tree to see him. When Jesus saw him, he said, "Zacchaeus, make haste and come down, for I must stay at your house today." He must have been surprised that Jesus noticed him and knew his name! He came down at once. The crowd complained that Jesus went to eat with sinners, because they viewed tax collectors for the Romans as Jewish traitors.

While Jesus was at his house, Zacchaeus stood and said, "Lord, the half of my goods I give to the poor; and if I have taken anything from any man by false accusation, I restore him fourfold." The commentaries are divided over whether this declaration is a promise or a practice. The verbs are in the present, not the future tense. Why did this chief tax collector want to see Jesus? Jericho was not far from where John the Baptist had been preaching. Had he heard John speak about Jesus? Was he among the tax collectors that had asked John, "What shall we do?" Did he repent upon hearing him say, "Exact no more than that which is appointed you"? (Luke 3:12-13) Could he have heard the parable of the tax collector who prayed, "God, be merciful to me a sinner"? (Luke 18:13) Zacchaeus may have already changed his ways, and out of gratitude he wanted to see Jesus and let him know what a difference he had made in his life. Yet, the Jews did not consider him "a son of Abraham" because he collected taxes for the Romans.

How did Jesus respond? He said, "Today salvation has come to this house, because he also is a son of Abraham; for the Son of Man has come to seek and to save that which was lost." Jesus is the Savior for all; even tax collectors for the Romans.

The Parable of the Ten Minas
Luke 19:11-28

Jesus told this parable, because he was near Jerusalem and his followers thought the kingdom of God would appear soon. They were expecting an immediate overthrow of the Romans. Jesus told the story of a nobleman that went to a far country to receive a kingdom. Before he left, he called his ten servants, and gave to each one a mina (or a pound). But the citizens of that realm hated him and sent a message, saying, "We will not have this man to reign over us." However, the nobleman received the kingdom in spite of their protest. When he returned, he called his servants to him to know how much each one had gained. One servant had gained ten more minas, and a second servant had gained five. But another one came with his one mina wrapped safely in a napkin. And the king commanded that the mina be taken from him and given to the one who had ten. And he said, "I tell you that to everyone who has, more will be given; but as for the one who has not, even what he has will be taken away." ᴱˢⱽ Then the king ordered the execution of his enemies that did not want him to reign over them.

The nobleman is Jesus Christ. His going into the far country is his ascension into heaven to receive a kingdom from God the Father. (Daniel 7:13-14) He is now reigning over his spiritual kingdom, the church. (Colossians 1:13-18) The Jews that rejected Jesus are the citizens of the realm who refused to recognize Jesus as their king. (John 19:15) All of Christ's servants are represented by the ten servants. The killing of the enemies is the judgment upon Jerusalem as a type of the eternal judgment. The return of the nobleman is the Second Coming of Christ.

When Jesus had said these things, he went on his way to Jerusalem.

NOTES

The Last Week

The Anointing at Bethany
John 12:1-8;
Matthew 26:6-13; Mark 14:3-9

Jesus came to Bethany, the hometown of Martha, Mary, and Lazarus, "six days before the Passover." Simon the leper hosted a supper on the Saturday evening before Jesus' Triumphal Entry into Jerusalem on Sunday. Matthew and Mark relate this story out of chronological order but in the context of Jesus speaking of his crucifixion and the Jewish leaders seeking to kill him. Jesus probably had healed Simon of his leprosy; and now he was honoring Jesus and celebrating the resurrection of Lazarus.

Martha served, and Mary anointed the head and feet of Jesus with a very costly oil of spikenard. Judas led the disciples in complaining that this was a waste; the oil could have been sold for three hundred denarii and given to the poor. Jesus said, "Let her alone; why trouble her? She has wrought a good work on me. For you have the poor always, and whenever you will you may do them good; but me you have not always. She has done what she could; she is come beforehand to anoint my body to the burying." This is the Mary who sat at Jesus' feet and heard his teachings in Luke 10:39. She seems to have been the only one listening to Jesus, when he said that he must suffer many things and be killed. Her anointing the body of Jesus was a beautiful act of faith, love, and devotion. What she did is still spoken of wherever the gospel is preached.

The Chief Priests Seek to Kill Lazarus
John 12:9-11

When the people knew that Jesus was in the house of Simon the leper, many came to see Lazarus as well as

Jesus. They wanted to see the man who had been dead for four days, but was now alive and well. Therefore, the chief priests wanted to kill Lazarus, because his resurrection was the reason many were now believing in Jesus. They were seeking to destroy the proof of Jesus' power.

The Triumphal Entry on Sunday
John 12:12-19; Matthew 21:1-11;
Mark 11:1-11; Luke 19:28-44

On the next day, Jesus entered Jerusalem from Bethany on the Mount of Olives riding on a donkey's colt upon which no one had ever sat. Matthew mentions a donkey and her colt. Solomon rode the mule of his father David when he was crowned king.[32] Matthew and John quote the prophecy of Zechariah 9:9, **"Behold, your King comes unto you, sitting upon a donkey, a colt, the foal of a donkey."**

When the people heard that Jesus was coming to Jerusalem, they went out to meet him, spreading their clothes and palm branches on the road. They were recognizing Jesus as their king, saying, "Hosanna to the Son of David." The Son of David would be the Messiah, the Christ. **Hosanna** means "Save now." (Psalm 118:25) They were quoting Psalm 118:26, "Blessed is he that comes in the name of the Lord," and saying, "Blessed is the kingdom of our father David." They were expecting Jesus to declare himself king over a political kingdom that would overthrow the Roman rule. But they would soon be disappointed in him. As Jesus came near to the city of Jerusalem, he wept as he predicted its destruction. After going into the temple and looking around, Jesus returned to Bethany with his apostles.

---

[32] 1 Kings 1:33

Jesus Curses the Fig Tree
Matthew 21:18-19; Mark 11:12-14

On his way to Jerusalem on Monday, Jesus cursed a fig tree that had leaves but no fruit. Immediately the fig tree withered away. Like the prophets, Jesus was acting out the parable of the barren fig tree in Luke 13:6-9.[33] The Jews were like a tree with an abundance of leaves but no fruit. He was warning of the judgment that was coming upon Jerusalem and was saying, "Have faith in God."

Jesus Cleanses the Temple on Monday
Mark 11:15-19; Matthew 21:12-17; Luke 19:45-46

On Monday, the day after the triumphal entry, Jesus went into the temple and drove out those that were buying and selling, and he overthrew the tables of the moneychangers. Jesus referred to Isaiah 56:7, saying, "My house shall be called a house of prayer for all nations." The Jews had made the temple of God "a den of thieves" just as their fathers had done in the days of Jeremiah. (Jeremiah 7:11)

Jesus' first act in Jerusalem after his triumphal entry was to cleanse the temple, which revealed the nature of his kingdom. As the Messiah, Jesus would use his power to cleanse men of sin—not to free them of the Romans.

After cleansing the temple, Jesus began to teach and to heal the blind and the lame that came to him in the temple. When evening came, he left Jerusalem. Jesus had cleansed the temple during the first year of his ministry, according to John 2:13-17. This shows how quickly men may go back to their old sinful ways; restoration is a constant need.

---

[33] Jeremiah 13 and Ezekiel 5

Jesus Taught Daily in the Temple
Luke 19:47-48; 21:37-38

Jesus taught daily in the temple, and the people were listening attentively to him. In the daytime Jesus was teaching in the temple, and his nights were on the Mount of Olives, where he had many friends, including Martha, Mary, and Lazarus at Bethany.

Jesus' Authority Questioned on Tuesday
Mark 11:27-33;
Matthew 21:23-27; Luke 20:1-8

Mark gives the time of this event: "And in the morning, they came again to Jerusalem." Matthew gives the setting: "And when he was come into the temple, he was teaching." Mark names all the accusers: "the chief priests, the scribes, and the elders." Matthew and Mark state their question: "By what authority do you these things? And who gave you this authority to do these things?"

They were questioning the authority for his cleansing the temple, his teaching, and his triumphal entry. Lewis states, "He had no rabbinical training, no hands had been laid on him, and he had no approval from the constituted authorities of the temple." [34]

Jesus said he would answer their question if they would answer his question. "The baptism of John, was it from heaven, or of men?" They would not answer this question. McMillan explains, "Their obvious purpose was to ensnare Jesus, and he cleverly escaped the trap. Yet his counter question was a veiled claim to heavenly authority." [35]

That same day, Jesus taught in parables.

---

[34] Jack P. Lewis, *The Gospel According to Matthew*, Part II, p. 90
[35] Earle McMillan, *The Gospel According to Mark*, p. 143

The Parable of the Wicked Vinedressers
Luke 20:9-19; Mark 12:1-12;
Matthew 21:33-46

In this parable, the landowner is God; his vineyard is the nation of Israel, the vinedressers are the rulers of Israel, his servants are the prophets, and his son is Jesus Christ. The landowner planted a vineyard and put vinedressers in charge of it, and then he went away. When he sent his servants to receive the fruit, they were beaten or killed. At last, he sent his son; and they killed him. Jesus then asked, "When the owner of the vineyard comes, what will he do to those vinedressers?" His audience said, "He will destroy those wicked men and will let out his vineyard to those that will give him the fruits in their seasons." Unknowingly, they condemned themselves.

Jesus then reminded them of the stone that the builders rejected becoming the chief cornerstone in Psalm 118:22-23. He said, "Therefore say I unto you, the kingdom of God shall be taken from you and given to a nation bringing forth the fruits thereof." That holy nation would be the church, the kingdom of God, consisting of believing Jews and Gentiles. (1 Peter 2:9-10)

When the chief priests and Pharisees heard this parable, they realized that he was speaking of them. They wanted to arrest Jesus, but they feared the people.

The Parable of the Two Sons
Matthew 21:28-32

A man had two sons. He said to the first, "Son, go work today in my vineyard." He answered, "I will not," but later he repented and went. The father said the same thing to his second son. And he answered, "I go, sir," but went not. Jesus asked, "Which one did the father's will?" They answered, "The first." Then Jesus said, "The tax collectors and the prostitutes go into the kingdom of God before you. For John came to you in the way of righteousness, and you did not believe him, but the tax collectors and the prostitutes believed him." ᴱˢⱽ

The Parable of the Wedding Feast
Matthew 22:1-14

The kingdom of heaven is like a wedding feast. God is the king, and Christ is the bridegroom. God's prophets are the servants. Jerusalem is the city that is burned. The wedding garment is Christ's righteousness, with which we are to be clothed. (Galatians 3:27) "Many are called, but few are chosen."

Is It Lawful to Pay Taxes to Caesar?
Matthew 22:15-22; Mark 12:13-17; Luke 20:20-26

The Pharisees and the Herodians (a political party allied with the Saducees) tried to trap Jesus with this question. Jesus asked whose image and inscription was on the Roman coin. They answered, "Caesar's." Then Jesus said, "Render to Caesar the things that are Caesar's, and to God the things that are God's." They marveled at his answer, but this was not what many of his followers wanted to hear. Christ's kingdom would be a spiritual one. He would not rebel against the Romans.

The Sadducees Question the Resurrection
Matthew 22:23-33; Mark 12:18-27; Luke 20:27-40

The Sadducees, who deny the resurrection of the dead, came to Jesus with a hypothetical story of a woman who had married seven brothers, each one dying before she married the next one. And at last, the woman died. Then they asked Jesus, "In the resurrection, whose wife shall she be of the seven? They all had her." Jesus answered, "You do err, not knowing the Scriptures, nor the power of God." He informed them that marriage will not exist in the resurrection, but we will be like the angels that do not marry. To prove the resurrection,

Jesus reminded them of what God had said to Moses at the burning bush: "I **am** the God of Abraham, and the God of Isaac, and the God of Jacob." Then Jesus made this necessary inference, "God is not the God of the dead, but of the living." Then some of the scribes said that Jesus had spoken well.

The Greatest Commandment
Matthew 22:34-40; Mark 12:28-34

A scribe, a man who knew the Law of Moses, asked Jesus, "Which is the first commandment of all?" Jesus answered, "'Thou shalt love the Lord thy God with all thy heart and with all thy soul, and with all thy mind, and with all thy strength.' This is the first commandment. And the second is like, namely this: 'Thou shalt love thy neighbor as thy self.'" When the scribe agreed with him, Jesus said to him, "You are not far from the kingdom of God."

Whose Son is the Christ
Matthew 22:41-46;
Mark 12:35-37; Luke 20:41-44

Jesus then had a question for the Pharisees, "What do you think about the Christ? Whose son is he?" "The son of David," they replied. He said to them, "How is it then that David, speaking by the Spirit, calls him 'Lord'? For he says, 'The Lord said to my Lord, "Sit at my right hand, until I put your enemies under your feet."' If then David calls him 'Lord,' how is he his son?" NIV David was being inspired by the Holy Spirit when he wrote these words in Psalm 110:1. The Christ would be more than a physical descendant of David; he would be a greater king than David. The Christ would be David's Lord. He would be the Son of God—a divine being.

Jesus Condemns the Hypocrisy of the Pharisees
Matthew 23:1-36;
Mark 12:38-40; Luke 20:45-47

Jesus condemned the scribes and Pharisees, calling them hypocrites, "for they say, and do not." They wanted to be seen of men and be called by religious titles. Jesus called them "blind guides." They had neglected the weightier matters of the law: justice and mercy and faith. He compared them to whited tombs, which appear beautiful on the outside, but within they are full of dead men's bones. Jesus asked rhetorically, "How can you escape the damnation of hell?"

Jesus would send prophets, and wise men, and scribes who would proclaim the gospel of the kingdom of God to them. But the scribes and Pharisees would kill and crucify some of them; they would scourge and persecute others from city to city. Jesus said, "All these things shall come upon this generation."

Jesus Laments over Jerusalem
Matthew 23:37-39

"O Jerusalem, Jerusalem, thou that kills the prophets and stones them which are sent unto you! How often I would have gathered your children together, even as a hen gathers her chickens under her wings, but you would not! Behold, your house is left unto you desolate. For I say unto you, you shall not see me henceforth, till you shall say, 'Blessed is he who comes in the name of the LORD!'"

Jesus Praises a Widow
Mark 12:41-44, Luke 21:1-4

Jesus had just condemned the scribes "who devour widows' houses." Now in contrast, he praises a widow for her sacrificial giving of two mites, "all that she had." These two mites were worth one sixty-fourth of a denarius, a day's wage for a laborer.³⁶ (Matthew 20:2) The Greek word for "mites" is *lepta,* and Mark explains in the Greek that two *lepta* make a *quadrans,* a Roman coin.³⁷ This is further proof that Mark is writing for a Roman audience.

Jesus Predicts the Destruction of the Temple
Luke 21:5-6; Mark 13:1-2;
Matthew 24:1-2

As Jesus was leaving the temple on Tuesday, some of the disciples spoke of the beautiful stones of the temple and its buildings. Jesus said, "There shall not be left one stone upon another that shall not be thrown down." Jesus was predicting the destruction of the temple and Jerusalem by the Romans that occurred in AD 70.

The Signs before the Destruction of Jerusalem
Matthew 24:3-34;
Luke 21:7-32; Mark 13:3-30

On their way back to Bethany on Tuesday afternoon, Jesus and his disciples rested on the west side of the Mount of Olives overlooking the city of Jerusalem. His apostles asked Jesus, "When shall these things be? And what shall be the sign when all these things shall be fulfilled?"

Jesus gave these signs for the destruction of the temple and the city of Jerusalem:

1. False prophets. (Matthew 24:4-5)
2. Wars and rumors of war. (Matthew 24:6-7)
3. Famines, pestilences, and earthquakes. (Matt. 24:7)
4. Persecution of Christ's disciples. (Matthew 24:9)
    "But he that shall endure unto the end, the same shall be saved." (Matthew 24:13)

---

³⁶ Earl McMillan, *The Gospel According to Mark*, p. 154
³⁷ David L. Roper, *The Life of Christ, 2,* p.318

5. The gospel of the kingdom shall be preached for a witness unto all nations. (Matthew 24:14)
6. The abomination in the temple. (Matthew 24:15-16)
   "When you therefore shall see the abomination of desolation, spoken of by Daniel the prophet, standing in the holy place ... flee."
7. Jerusalem will be surrounded by armies.
   "When you see Jerusalem being surrounded by armies you know that its destruction is near." (Luke 21:20, NKJV)

These signs would be in the first century before the destruction of Jerusalem in AD 70. Jesus said, "I say unto you, that this generation shall not pass away till all these things be done." (Mark 13:30)

The Coming of Christ and the End of the World
Mark 13:31-37; Luke 21:33-38;
Matthew 24: 35-51

Jesus said, "Heaven and earth shall pass away, but my words shall not pass away. But of that day and hour knows no man, no, not the angels which are in heaven, neither the Son, but the Father. Take heed, watch and pray, for you know not when the time is." (Mark 13:31-32) There will be no signs before Christ's second coming. He is coming as a thief—unexpected. (2 Peter 3:10)

The Parable of the Wise and Foolish Virgins
Matthew 25:1-13

The ten virgins represent the church as it anticipates the coming of Christ, the bridegroom. The five wise virgins made sufficient preparation, but the five foolish virgins did not. Both groups made some preparation; they all brought lamps. But the foolish did not bring additional oil. More than initial faith is needed, according to 2 Peter 1:5-11. The delay of the bridegroom suggests that the time of Christ's coming is not known. Death is represented by the sleep of the virgins.

After death it is too late to prepare for his coming. Jesus said, "Watch therefore, for you know neither the day nor the hour wherein the Son of man comes." This is the first of three parables illustrating our need to be prepared for Christ's coming and the judgment.

The Parable of the Talents
Matthew 25:14-30

Christ's ascension to heaven is like a man going to a far country, who called his servants and gave his goods to them. Christ has entrusted the gospel to his disciples. One servant received five talents, another two, and another one; to each one according to his ability. The first two servants went out and doubled their talents; but he that received one buried his talent in the ground for safe keeping. After a long time, the master returned. He had equal praise and reward for the two faithful servants that had doubled their talents. He said to each one, "Well done, good and faithful servant. Enter into the joy of your lord." But to the one who had buried his talent, he said, "You wicked, lazy servant!" NIV And he was cast into outer darkness, where there was weeping and gnashing of teeth. Each Christian must be faithful in spreading the gospel, according to his ability, while waiting for the Lord's return.

The Parable of the Sheep and the Goats
Matthew 25:31-46

As a shepherd separates his sheep from the goats by placing the sheep on his right hand and the goats on the left, so Christ will separate the blessed from the cursed, when he comes in his glory with all his holy angels at the end of time.

He will sit on his great white throne of judgment after this earth and the heavens have passed away. (Rev. 20:11) All nations will be gathered before him. Every person that has ever lived will be judged. Those on his right hand will be those that have ministered to him with benevolent acts to others. Those on the left will be those that have failed to do so.

He will say to those on his right hand, "Come, you blessed of my Father, inherit the kingdom prepared for you from the foundation of the world. For I was hungry, and you gave me food. I was thirsty, and you gave me drink. I was sick, and you visited me. I was in prison, and you came to me." Then the righteous will say, "Lord, when did we do these things for you?" And the King will say to them, "Inasmuch as you have done it unto one of the least of these my brethren, you have done it unto me."

But he will say to those on his left hand he, "Depart from me, you cursed, into everlasting fire, prepared for the devil and his angels. Inasmuch as you did it not to one of the least of these, you did it not to me."

And these shall go away into everlasting punishment, but the righteous into eternal life.

We must minister to the needs of our brethren.

The Time of the Passover
Matthew 26:1-2; Mark 14:1; Luke 22:1

On Tuesday afternoon, Jesus was with his apostles on the Mount of Olives overlooking the temple in Jerusalem. When Jesus had finished speaking about the destruction of Jerusalem and his second coming, he said to his disciples, "You know that **after two days is the feast of the Passover**, and the Son of Man is betrayed to be crucified." Two days from Tuesday afternoon would be Thursday.

The traditional view is that Jesus was crucified on Friday with the Passover being on Saturday; and on Sunday, he was raised from the dead. Most harmonies of the gospels have Jesus doing nothing on Wednesday. However, "He was teaching daily in the temple," according to Luke 19:47 and 21:37.

F. LaGard Smith asks, "In an action-packed final week, what reason is there to believe that there would be a whole day of either inactivity or activity which is left unrecorded? Second, and far more important—if Jesus is crucified on Friday afternoon and thereafter hurriedly put in the tomb, how can there be sufficient time to match Jesus' own prediction that he would remain in the tomb for three days and three nights before his resurrection? The resolution of both questions appears to be found in recognizing that the last supper took place on Wednesday evening, followed by the crucifixion and burial on Thursday." [38]

Jesus was crucified on the day of the preparation for the Passover. (John 19:14) The Passover was on a day of rest (Exodus 12:16) called a "high day" sabbath in John 19:31. Jesus died on Thursday, the day before the Passover on Friday, followed by the weekly Sabbath on Saturday. He was raised from the dead on Sunday, after two sabbaths: the Passover sabbath and the weekly sabbath. The Greek word for sabbath in Matthew 28:1 is plural, ***sabbaths***.[39] Burton Coffman became convinced that the crucifixion was on Thursday by Roger Rusk in *Christianity Today,* March 29, 1974; Rusk proved that the Passover was on Friday the year that Jesus was crucified. [40]

The Plot to Kill Jesus
Luke 22:2, Mark 14:1-2, Matthew 26:3-5

The chief priests, the scribes, and elders were looking for a way to arrest and kill Jesus. On Tuesday evening, they met in the palace of the high priest trying to come up with a plan to kill Jesus before the Passover.

---

[38] F. LaGard Smith, *The Narrated Bible,* p. 1454
[39] *Sabbath* means cessation from labor, rest.
[40] James Burton Coffman, *Coffman's Bible Commentary,* Mark 15:42

Greeks Seek Jesus
John 12:20-22

While Jesus was teaching in the temple on Wednesday, some God-fearing Greeks said to Philip, "Sir, we would see Jesus." Greeks were allowed only to be in the Court of the Gentiles, and they were requesting that Jesus come to them. Philip and Andrew told Jesus that some Greeks were seeking him. Jesus knew that his mission was to die for the sins of all men, including the Gentiles. Therefore, Jesus answered…

"The Hour Is Come"
John 12:23-33

Earlier, Jesus stated that his hour or time had not yet come. (John 2:4; 7:6,8,30; 8:20) Now, Jesus boldly states, "The hour is come that the Son of Man should be glorified." He is speaking of his dying for our sins and his being raised for our justification. (Romans 4:24-25)

Jesus revealed that his soul was troubled; but he declared, "For this cause, I came unto this hour." Then he prayed, "Father, glorify thy name." And a voice from heaven answered, "I have both glorified it, and will glorify it again." Jesus stated, "Now the prince of this world shall be cast out. And I, if I be lifted up from the earth, will draw all men unto me." He was speaking of his crucifixion.

The Light of Jesus
John 12:34-36

The people were expecting the Christ to have a long earthly reign. They were perplexed by his saying he would be glorified by death. He said to them, "Yet a little while is the light with you. Walk while you have the light, lest darkness come upon you. While you have the light, believe in the light, that you may be the children of light." When he said these things, Jesus left and hid himself from them.

Jesus Fulfilled Isaiah 53
John 12:37-43

"Even after Jesus had done all these miraculous signs in their presence, they still would not believe in him. This was to fulfill the word of Isaiah the prophet: 'Lord, who has believed our message and to whom has the arm of the Lord been revealed?' For this reason, they could not believe." ᴺᴵⱽ Because they **would not** believe, their hearts became so hardened that they **could not** believe. Among the chief rulers many believed in Jesus; but they would not confess him, because they did not want to be put out of the synagogue; for they loved the praise of men more than the praise of God. Jesus had said, "Whoever shall deny me before men, him will I also deny before my Father who is in heaven." (Matthew 10:33) James would write: "Faith, if it has not works, is dead being alone." (James 2:17) The Holy Spirit says, "Today, if you will hear his voice, harden not your hearts." (Hebrews 3:7) We may so harden our hearts that it will be impossible for us to repent, according to Hebrews 6:4-6.

The Final Words of Jesus to the People
John 12:44-50

On the final day of his teaching the people, Jesus cried out and said, "He that believes in me, believes not in me, but in him who sent me." **"He that rejects me and receives not my words has one that judges him; the word I have spoken, the same shall judge him in the last day.** For I have not spoken of myself; but the Father who sent me, he gave me a commandment, what I should say, and what I should speak. And I know that his commandment is life everlasting."

Judas Agrees to Betray Jesus
Matthew 26:14-16, Mark 14:10-11, Luke 22:3-6

Then one of the twelve, called Judas Iscariot, went to the chief priests and said to them, "What will you give me, and I will deliver him to you?" The Jewish leaders were glad to hear this. They could arrest Jesus in a private place without creating an uproar among the people. And they agreed on thirty pieces of silver.

The Last Supper

Luke 22:7-16;
Mark 14:12-17; Matthew 26:17-20

Jesus ate the Last Supper with his apostles after sundown on Wednesday evening. (Jewish days began at sundown.) The first day of the feast of unleavened bread, Nisan 14, began that year at sundown on Wednesday. (Exodus 12:1-8) The killing of the Passover lambs began at 3 p.m. on Thursday, Nisan 14. Jesus died at 3 p.m. on Thursday as our Passover Lamb. (1 Cor. 5:7)

F. LaGard Smith says, "Jesus seems to explain why it is important for him to eat with them on the night before the actual Passover meal. Jesus' words are 'I have eagerly desired to eat this Passover with you before I suffer. For I tell you, I will not eat it again until it finds fulfillment in the kingdom of God.' In referring to his suffering, Jesus is obviously anticipating that his own sacrificial death will take place later that day, preventing him from participating in the actual Passover supper. John's account eliminates any doubt that this supper occurred prior to the actual Passover meal. When Jesus tells Judas during the supper to do what he is about to do, some of the other disciples thought Jesus was telling him to buy what was needed for the Feast. (John 13:27-29) Most convincing is the fact that the day of Jesus' crucifixion is plainly stated to be 'the day of Preparation of Passover Week'—the day on which the pascal lamb is slain for the Passover meal taken during the evening of that day." [41] (Read John 19:31 and 42)

---

[41] F. LaGard Smith, *The Narrated Bible*, p. 1455

Jesus Institutes the Lord's Supper
Matthew 26:26-29; Mark 14:22-25; Luke 22:17-20

Jesus took bread, and blessed it, and broke off a piece to eat, and gave it to the apostles and said, "Take, eat; this is my body." And he took the cup, and gave thanks, and said, "Drink ye all of it. For this is my blood of the new testament, which is shed for many for the remission of sins." Jesus said, "Do this in remembrance of me." He promised, "I will drink no more of the fruit of the vine, until I drink it new in the kingdom of God."

Jesus Would Be Betrayed
Luke 22:21-23; Mark 14:18

Jesus revealed that someone with him at the table would betray him. And the apostles began questioning among themselves who would do such a thing.

Strife over Greatness in the Kingdom
Luke 22:24-28

Also, there was strife among the apostles about which one of them would be greatest in the kingdom. Jesus' reference to the kingdom of God may have prompted this discussion. Jesus informed them the chief among them would be the one who serves. And he gave himself as an example.

The Apostles Would Judge Israel
Luke 22:29-30

Jesus promised his apostles a kingdom, and they would sit on thrones judging the twelve tribes of Israel. They were given this kingdom on the day of Pentecost, and they convicted the Jews of crucifying the One whom God had made both Lord and Christ. (Acts 2:1-36)

Jesus Washes His Apostles' Feet
John 13:1-17

Verse one plainly states that this supper was before the Passover feast. After the Last Supper, Jesus washed the feet of his apostles. Jesus could render this lowly service, because he knew who he was and that he was going to God the Father in heaven. Because Peter could not stand the thought of Jesus humbling himself in this way, he said to him, "You will never wash my feet." But when Jesus answered, "If I do not wash you, you will have no part with me," Peter replied, "Lord, not my feet only, but also my hands and head." Jesus answered that only dirty feet needed to be washed. This shows that Jesus was not instituting the "foot washing service" that some practice. Jesus said, "I have given you an example, that you should do **as** I have done." He even washed the feet of Judas, who would betray him. As Christians, we should be willing to render the most-humble service to others, even for our enemies. We can serve others, when we also know who we are and where we are going.

Jesus Reveals Who Would Betray Him
John 13:18-30; Matthew 26:20-25; Mark 14:19-21

After washing their feet, Jesus said one of his apostles would fulfill Psalm 41:9, "He who eats bread with me has lifted up his heel against me." Then he plainly said one of the apostles would betray him. John reclining next to him whispered, "Lord, who is it?" Jesus said, "It is he to whom I shall give a piece of bread." Having dipped the bread, he gave it to Judas. Judas asked, "Master, is it I?" He quietly answered, "You have said it. What you do, do quickly." Some of the apostles thought that Jesus was sending Judas to get those things needed for the feast. But Judas went out into the night to arrange the betrayal of Jesus.

A New Commandment
John 13:31-35

When Judas had gone out, Jesus said, "Now the Son of Man is glorified, and God is glorified in him ... Little children, yet a little while I am with you ... A new commandment I give unto you, that you love one another as I have loved you; that you also love one another." Jesus made an old commandment new by adding "as I have loved you." He is the perfect example of love.

Jesus Predicts Peter Would Deny Him
John 13:36-38; Luke 22:31-34,
Mark 14:27-31; Matthew 26:31-35

Peter asked Jesus where he was going, and Jesus said that where he was going Peter could not follow him immediately. Peter asked, "Why can't I follow you now? I will lay down my life for you." Jesus answered, "Will you lay down your life for my sake? Simon, Simon! Satan has desired to have you, that he may sift you as wheat. But I have prayed for you. When you are converted, strengthen your brethren."

And Peter said, "Lord, I am ready to go with you, both to prison and to death." Then Jesus said to his apostles, "All ye shall be offended because of me this night. But after I am risen, I will go before you into Galilee."

But Peter said to him, "Although all shall be offended, yet I will not." And Jesus said to him, "I say to you, that this day, even this night, before the cock crows twice, you shall deny me three times." But Peter said vehemently, "If I should die with you, I will not deny you in any way." And all the apostles said the same thing.

"Let Not Your Heart Be Troubled"
John 14:1-3

The apostles were troubled when they heard the words of Jesus that he was going away and they would all be offended because of him. So, Jesus said, "Let not your heart be troubled; believe in God, believe also in Me. In My Father's house are many dwelling places; if it were not so, I would have told you; for I go to prepare a place for you. And if I go and prepare a place for you, I will come again, and receive you to Myself; that where I am, there you may be also." NASB Faith is the cure for a troubled heart.

Jesus Is the Way, the Truth and the Life
John 14:4-6

When Jesus said, "You know where I go; and you know the way," Thomas said, "Lord, we do not know where you are going, and how can we know the way?" Jesus answered, "I am the way, the truth, and the life. No one comes to the Father, except through Me." NKJV

Knowing the Father
John 14:7-11

Jesus then told his apostles that if they had known him, they would have known the Father. They had seen the Father in the life of Jesus.

Philip said to him, "Show us the Father." Jesus replied, "Have I been so long time with you, and yet you have not known me, Philip? He that has seen me has seen the Father." They are not the same person, but they both possess the same divine nature and attributes. The words that Jesus spoke were the words of the Father; and the works that Jesus did were the works of the Father.

The Father Would Continue His Work
John 14:12-14

Jesus was speaking to his apostles when he said, "He that believes on me, the works that I do he will do also, and greater works than these he shall do also, because I go unto my Father." In the book of Acts, we read of the apostles performing the same types of miracles that Jesus did. The "greater works" were the words inspired by God that brought salvation to lost mankind through the preaching of the gospel of Christ. God continues to work in answering prayers in the name of Jesus.

Jesus Promises Another Helper
John 14:15-24

Jesus said, "If you love me, keep my commandments. And I will pray the Father, and he shall give you another Comforter, that he may abide with you forever—even the Spirit of truth." The world will not know the Comforter; but Christ's disciples will know him, for he will dwell with them. Jesus said that he would soon go away and his apostles would not see him, but they would see him again. He was referring to his death and resurrection. He then promised, "Because I live, you shall live also." He who has Christ's commandments and keeps them is the one who loves him; and the Father and the Son will love him and dwell with him.

The Gift of the Holy Spirit
John 14:25-26

Jesus was going away, but the Father would send the Holy Spirit, who would teach the apostles all things, and bring to their remembrance all things that Jesus had said to them. Because of the gift of the Holy Spirit, we have the new covenant of Christ, including his life and teachings. Therefore, we have the Spirit of truth abiding with us forever in the pages of the New Testament. Jesus had said, "My words shall not pass away." (Matthew 24:35) Peter later wrote, "His divine power has given unto us all things that pertain to life and godliness, through the knowledge of him." (2 Peter 1:3)

Christ Gives His Peace
John 14:27-31;
Luke 22:35-38; Matthew 26:30

Jesus concluded with these words of encouragement: "Peace I leave with you, my peace I give unto you; not as the world gives, I give unto you. Let not your heart be troubled, neither let it be afraid."

Then Jesus asked them, "When I sent you without purse, and wallet. and shoes, lacked you anything?" And they said, "Nothing." Then he said, "But now, he that has a purse, let him take it, and likewise his wallet; and he that has no sword, let him sell his garment, and buy one." Jesus was preparing his disciples for his crucifixion and for the persecutions that they would face.

They said, "Lord, here are two swords." And he said to them, "It is enough." Two swords would be enough for him to use in order to teach them an important lesson later that evening. One belonged to Peter.

"And when they had sung a hymn, they went out into the mount of Olives."

NOTES

Wednesday Evening

The Vine and the Branches
John 15:1-8

On their way to the Mount of Olives, Jesus taught his disciples an important lesson, saying, "I am the true vine and my Father is the husbandman. Every branch in me that bears not fruit he takes away, and every branch that bears fruit, he purges it, that it may bring forth more fruit." Jesus is teaching the importance of our abiding in him. He said, "For without me, you can do nothing." We are purged, or made clean, through the words of Christ. The heavenly Father is glorified when we bear much fruit. Jesus said, "If a man abides not in me, he is cast forth as a branch, and is withered; and men gather them and cast them into the fire, and they are burned."

Abiding in Christ's Love
John 15:9-12

The Father has loved Jesus, and Jesus has loved us. We are to continue in his love, by keeping his commandments. Jesus said, "These things I have spoken unto you, that my joy might remain in you, and that your joy might be full. This is my commandment, that you love one another, as I have loved you."

"You Are My Friends"
John 15:13-17

Jesus told his disciples, "Greater love has no man than this, that a man lay down his life for his friends. You are my friends, if you do whatever I command you." Jesus had made known to his friends all things he had heard from his Father. He had chosen them to bring forth fruit—others who would obey God. The Father would give to them whatever they asked in the name of Jesus. The friends of Jesus are to love each other.

The World's Hatred
John 15:18-25

Jesus said, "If the world hates you, you know that it hated me before it hated you. If you were of the world, the world would love his own; but because you are not of the world, but I have chosen you out of the world, therefore the world hates you. Remember the word that I said unto you. The servant is not greater than his lord. If they have persecuted me, they will also persecute you; if they have kept my saying, they will keep yours also." The world persecutes Christ and his disciples, because they do not know God the Father.

Knowledge and Responsibility
John 15:22-25

Jesus taught that knowledge and opportunity bring with them responsibility. He said, "If I had not come and spoken unto them, they had not had sin; but now they have no cloak for their sin. He that hates me hates my Father also. If I had not done among them the works which none other man did, they had not had sin. But now they have both seen and hated both me and my Father." Jesus fulfilled the old covenant Scriptures, "They hated me without a cause." (Psalm 35:19; Psalm 69:4)

The Holy Spirit and the Apostles Will Testify
John 15:26-27

Jesus predicted, "But when the Comforter is come, whom I will send to you from the Father, even the Spirit of truth, who proceeds from the Father, he shall testify of me. And you also shall bear witness, because you have been with me from the beginning." The apostles were chosen, because they had been with Jesus from the beginning of his ministry. (Acts 1:21-26)

Jesus Prepares His Disciples for Persecution
John 16:1-4

Jesus tells his apostles that the Jews would put them out of their synagogues; and the time would come if someone kills them, he will think that he has done a service to God. Saul of Tarsus felt he was serving God when he persecuted Christians. When persecutions come, we are to remember that Jesus had predicted them. "All that will live godly in Christ shall suffer persecution." (2 Timothy 3:12) So, we should not be surprised when we suffer for our faith.

Jesus Must Go Away
John 16:5-11

Jesus must return to the heavenly Father. The hearts of his disciples were filled with sorrow when they heard him say this. It was necessary for him to go away, so he could send the Comforter, the Holy Spirit, who would reprove the world of sin, and of righteousness, and of judgment.

The Guidance of the Holy Spirit
John 16:12-15

Jesus had many things to say to his disciples, but they were not prepared to understand them at that time. However, he would send the Holy Spirit, the Spirit of truth, who would guide them into all truth. The Spirit would not speak of himself, but he would glorify Jesus by revealing his words. The words of the inspired writers of the New Testament are the words of Jesus just as much as those in red letters in your Bible. This is the gift of the Holy Spirit. If the Holy Spirit had not come upon the apostles, we would not have the New Testament, which reveals Christ and his teachings. Paul wrote, "When you read, you may understand my knowledge in the mystery of Christ, which in other ages was not made known unto the sons of men, as it is now revealed unto his holy apostles and prophets by the

Spirit." (Ephesians 3:4-5) God the Father gave these words to Jesus, and he revealed them through the Spirit to his apostles and prophets. This confirms the doctrine of the Trinity. The Spirit is not revealing any new truths today. His mission has been completed. (2 Peter 1:3) The Spirit abides with us within the pages of the New Testament.

The Apostles Were Confused
John 16:16-19

The apostles were perplexed when Jesus said, "A little while, and you shall not see me; and again, a little while, and you shall see me, because I go to the Father." What did he mean? He was speaking of his death, resurrection, and ascension.

Jesus Tells of His Death and Resurrection
John 16:20-24

Jesus' death would be like a woman's suffering during childbirth, and his resurrection would be like her joy when her baby is born. He said, "And you now therefore have sorrow; but I will see you again, and your joy no man takes from you." After his resurrection, they would be able to pray to the Father in Jesus' name, and their joy would be full.

Jesus Tells of His Return to the Father
John 16:25-30

Jesus plainly tells his apostles that he came forth from the Father in heaven and is now in the world, but he would leave the world and return to the Father. His disciples confessed that Jesus knows all things and that he came from the Father.

The Apostles Would Be Scattered
John 16:31-32

Jesus asked his apostles, "Do you now believe?" He then predicts that they would be scattered and leave him alone, but the Father would be with him through his trials. It would happen that very night. They would not fully believe until he was resurrected from the dead.

Jesus Overcomes the World
John 16:33

Jesus had told them distressful things that night; but in time, they would have peace in him. Christians will have sufferings in the world; but they should rejoice, because Jesus has overcome the world. The victory is in Jesus!

Jesus Prays to the Father
John 17:1

This prayer was made before they crossed the brook Kidron and entered the garden of Gethsemane. (18:1) Jesus looking up into heaven said, "Father, the hour is come. Glorify your Son, that your Son also may glorify you." The time had come for Jesus to fulfill his purpose for coming into the world. He came to die for our sins and to be resurrected from the dead in order to establish the eternal kingdom of God and reign as King of kings under the new covenant. The prophecies of God would be fulfilled. God the Father would be glorified when he gloried Jesus.

Jesus Brings Eternal Life
John 17:2-3

Eternal life is given to those who know the Father and Jesus Christ, whom he has sent. This knowledge comes through experiencing a close relationship with the only true God—loving and obeying him.

Jesus Prays for Himself
John 17:4-5

Jesus had glorified God the Father during his ministry by his compassion, his miracles and his teachings. Jesus will now complete his work of atonement and resurrection. He was so totally committed to his mission that he could say, "I have finished the work which you gave me to do. And now, O Father, glorify me with your own glory which I had with you before the world was." Jesus longed for the glorious relationship that he had with the Father in eternity before he came to earth.

Jesus Prays for His Disciples
John 17:6-19

The disciples of Jesus knew that he came from the Father and that his teachings were words from God. Jesus said, "I pray for them ... I am glorified in them ... And now I am no more in the world, but these are in the world ... Holy Father, keep through your own name those whom you have given me ... that they might have my joy fulfilled in themselves ... Sanctify them through your truth; your word is truth ... As you have sent me into the world, even so I have also sent them into the world."

Jesus Prays for the Unity of Believers
John 17:20-23

Jesus said that he was praying not only for his apostles, but also for those who would believe in him through their word. He prayed that all believers would be one, even as He and the Father are one; so that the world may believe that the Father had sent him.

Jesus Wants Us to be with Him
John 17:24-26

"Father, I will that they also, whom you have given me, be with me where I am, that they may behold my glory, which you have given me; for you loved me before the foundation of the world." Jesus wants us with him in heaven to see his glory. He wants us to experience his love and share it with others.

Jesus Enters the Garden of Gethsemane
John 18:1; Mark 14:32-34; Matthew 26:36-38

When Jesus had spoken these words, he went over the brook Kidron with his apostles and entered the Garden of Gethsemane on the Mount of Olives. And he said to his disciples, "Sit here, while I pray." And he took with him Peter and James and John. Then Jesus said to these three apostles, "My soul is exceedingly sorrowful unto death; tarry here and watch."

Jesus Falls on His Face and Prays
Matthew 26:39-46; Mark 14:35-42; Luke 22:39-46

And he went a little farther and fell on his face and prayed, saying, "O my Father, if it be possible, let this cup pass from me; nevertheless, not as I will, but as you will. Abba, Father, all things are possible to you; take away this cup from me: nevertheless, not as I will, but what you will." There appeared to him an angel from heaven, strengthening him. When he returned to the three, he found them sleeping, and said, "What, could you not watch with me one hour? Watch and pray that you enter not into temptation; the spirit is willing, but the flesh is weak." He went away again the second time, and prayed, saying, "O my Father, if this cup may not pass away from me, except I drink it, your will be done." And Jesus came to the three and found them asleep again, for their eyes were heavy. So, he left them, and being in agony, he prayed the third time more earnestly saying the same words. Then his sweat became like great drops of blood falling down to the ground. After praying, Jesus was filled with strength to face his trials and the cross. Returning to his apostles he boldly said, "The hour has come; behold, the Son of Man is being betrayed into the hands of sinners. Rise, let us be going. See, My betrayer is at hand." NKJV

Jesus Is Betrayed and Arrested
Mark 14:43-49; John 18:2-12;
Matthew 26:47-56; Luke 22:47-53

Immediately, while Jesus was still speaking, Judas came with a great multitude. Judas knew the place where Jesus would be, because he often came there with his disciples. Judas received a detachment of soldiers, who came with lanterns, torches, and weapons. Jesus asked, "Whom do you seek?" And they said, "Jesus of Nazareth." Jesus boldly said, "I am he." When he said this, they fell backward to the ground. Then he asked again, "Whom do you seek?" And they said, "Jesus of Nazareth." Jesus answered, "I have told you that I am he; if therefore you seek me, let these go their way." Jesus did not want to lose any of his apostles. Judas had given the soldiers a signal, that Jesus would be the one he kissed. He came to Jesus and said, "Master, master," and kissed him. Jesus said to him, "Judas, are you betraying the Son of Man with a kiss?"

When they laid their hands on Jesus, Peter drew his sword and struck Malchus, the servant of the high priest, cutting off his right ear. Then Jesus said to Peter, "Put your sword back into its place. For all who take the sword will perish by the sword." Jesus said he could pray to his Father, and he would send him more than twelve legions of angels. Jesus asked rhetorically, "Shall I not drink the cup which my Father has given me?" Earlier, Peter had said, "Lord, I am ready to go with you, both to prison and to death." He and the other apostles were ready to fight to the death for Jesus and his kingdom. Seeking an occasion to teach them about the nature of his kingdom, Jesus told them to get a sword. They revealed that they had two swords. (Luke 22:31-38) It would be enough to teach them the lessons he wanted them to learn. He was fulling the Scriptures; he was being led "as a lamb to the slaughter." (Isaiah 53:7)

Showing his peaceable nature and power, Jesus restored the ear that had been cut off. Then Jesus said to the chief priests, captains of the temple, and the elders who had come to him, "Are you come out as against a thief, with swords and clubs? When I was daily with you in the temple, you stretched forth no hands against me; but this is your hour and the power of darkness." Jesus was the one in control; everything was going according to God's plan. All these things were in fulfillment of prophecies in the Holy Scriptures. Then the Jewish officials with the Roman soldiers arrested Jesus.

His Disciples Forsake Him
Matthew 26:56; Mark 14:50-52; Luke 22:54

Then all the disciples forsook Jesus and fled. "And there followed him a certain young man, having a linen cloth cast about his naked body, and the young men laid hold on him; and he left the linen cloth and fled from them naked." ^{Mark} Some believe this young man was John Mark, because his gospel account is the only one that mentions this event. [42] Peter followed at a distance. ^{Luke}

---

[42] Earle McMillian, *The Gospel According to Mark*, p. 175

NOTES

The Trials

Jesus before Annas
John 18:13-14; 19-23

Jesus was taken to Annas, a former high priest, who was influential among the Jews. Annas asked Jesus about his disciples and his teachings. Jesus said he had spoken openly and taught in the synagogues and in the temple; he had done nothing in secret. He should not have to testify to what he had done; there were many witnesses, which the Jewish legal procedures required.[43] Then one of the officers struck Jesus with the palm of his hand for answering the high priest in this way. Jesus said to him, "If I have spoken evil, bear witness of the evil; but if well, why do you strike me?"

Peter's First Denial of Jesus
John 18:15-18;
Matthew 26:69-70; Mark 14:66-68

Peter and John followed Jesus to the house of Annas. (John never refers to himself by his name in his writings) John was known to the high priest; so he was able to enter the courtyard. John spoke to the doorkeeper and brought Peter in. Later, the maid who kept the door said to Peter as they were warming themselves by a fire, "You are not also one of this man's disciples, are you?" He said, "I am not." [NASB] Then recognizing him she said, "You also were with Jesus of Galilee." But he denied it before them all, saying, "I do not know what you are saying." [Matthew] Peter then went out on the porch, and a rooster crowed. [Mark]

---

[43] Frank Pack, *The Gospel According to John, Part II*, p. 117

Jesus before Caiaphas
John 18:24; Matthew 26:57-59

Annas then sent Jesus to Caiaphas the high priest. The Romans had replaced Annas as high priest with his son-in-law, Caiaphas. The soldiers led him away to Caiaphas' house, where the chief priests, the elders and the scribes were assembled. Peter followed at a distance to the courtyard of Caiaphas and sat down with the servants and warmed himself by the fire.

Peter Denies Jesus Three Times
Matthew 26: 71-75; Mark 14:69-72;
John 18:25-27; Luke 22:58-62;

After a little while during the trial of Jesus at the house of Caiaphas, another girl saw Peter and said, "This fellow also was with Jesus of Nazareth." And the servant girl who had first accused Peter saw him again and said, "This is one of them." But he denied it again with an oath, saying, "I do not know the man!" Then after an hour had passed, another affirmed, "Surely, this fellow was also with him, for he is a Galilean." One of the servants of the high priests, a relative of him whose ear Peter had cut off, said, "Did I not see you in the garden with him?" Those who stood by said to Peter, "Surely you also are one of them, for your speech betrays you." Then Peter began to curse and swear, saying, "I do not know the man!" Immediately, while he was still speaking, the rooster crowed. And the Lord turned and looked at him. Then Peter recalled the words of Jesus, how he had said to him, "Before the rooster crows twice, you will deny me three times." Mark 14:30 So Peter went out and wept bitterly.

Jesus is Mocked and Beaten
Luke 22:63-65

The men who held Jesus mocked and beat him. They blindfolded him, and struck him with the palms of their hands, saying, "Prophesy to us Christ! Who is the one who struck you?" They spoke many words of blasphemy against him.

Jesus Is Condemned by the Sanhedrin
Luke 22:66-71;
Matthew 26:59-68; Mark 14:55-68

As soon as it was day, the elders of the people, both chief priests and scribes, came together and led Jesus into their council, saying, "If you are the Christ, tell us." But he said, "If I tell you, you will by no means believe." All the council of the Jews sought testimony against Jesus to put him to death, but found none. At last, two false witnesses testified that Jesus had said, "I am able to destroy the temple of God, and to build it in three days." But even then, they did not agree in their testimony. The high priest asked Jesus, "Do you answer nothing? What is it these men testify against you?" But Jesus kept silent. Then the high priest said to him, "I put you under oath by the living God. Tell us if you are the Christ, the Son of God!"

Jesus said to him, "It is as you said. Nevertheless, I say to you, hereafter you will see the Son of Man sitting at the right hand of the Power, and coming in the clouds of heaven."

Then the high priest tore his clothes, saying, "He has spoken blasphemy. What further need do we have of witnesses? Behold, now you have heard his blasphemy. What do you think?" They answered, "He is guilty of death." Then the council members spat in his face, and buffeted him.

Judas Hangs Himself
Matthew 27:3-10

When Judas saw that Jesus had been condemned to die, he was filled with remorse and returned the thirty pieces of silver to the chief priests and elders, saying, "I have sinned by betraying innocent blood." And he threw down the pieces of silver in the temple and went out and hanged himself. Because the silver was blood money, they could not put it back into the treasury. So, they bought a potter's field, in which to bury strangers. This was in fulfillment of a prophecy that was spoken by Jeremiah and recorded in Zechariah 11:12-13.

Jesus before Pilate
Matthew 27:1-2, 11-14; Mark 15:1-5;
John 18:28-38; Luke 23:1-7

Then they led Jesus from Caiaphas to the Praetorium, and it was early morning. But the Jews themselves did not go into the Praetorium, lest they should be defiled, due to the Passover. Pilate then went out to them and said, "What accusation do you bring against this man?" They said, "If he were not a criminal, we would not have delivered him up to you." And they began to accuse him saying, "We found this fellow perverting the nation, and forbidding to pay taxes to Caesar, saying that he himself is Christ a King." And the chief priests accused Jesus of many things, but he answered nothing. Pilate asked Jesus, "Do you answer nothing? See how many things they testify against you!" But Jesus still answered nothing, so that Pilate marveled. Then Pilate said to them, "You take him and judge him according to your law." The Jews said, "It is not lawful for us to put anyone to death." They could not put anyone to death by crucifixion.

Then Pilate entered the governor's headquarters again, and called for Jesus to be brought before him. He asked Jesus, "Are you the King of the Jews?" Jesus answered, "My kingdom is not of this world. If my kingdom were of this world, my servants would fight, so that I should not be delivered to the Jews; but now my kingdom is not from here." Pilate therefore said to him, "Are you a king then?" Jesus answered, "You say rightly that I am a king. For this cause, I was born, and for this cause, I have come into the world, that I should bear witness to the truth. Everyone who is of the truth hears my voice." Pilate said to him, "What is truth?"

Pilate then went out again to the Jews and said to them, "I find not fault in him." But they shouted out, "He stirs up the people, teaching throughout all Judea, beginning from Galilee to this place. "When Pilate heard of Galilee, he asked if Jesus was a Galilean. As soon as he knew that Jesus belonged to Herod's jurisdiction, he sent him to Herod, who was also in Jerusalem at that time.

Jesus before Herod
Luke 23:8-12

When Herod saw Jesus, he was glad, because he had desired for a long time to see him. He had heard many things about him, and he hoped to see some miracle. Herod asked Jesus many questions, but he answered him nothing. The chief priests and scribes brought accusations against Jesus. Then Herod and his soldiers treated Jesus with contempt. They put a gorgeous robe on him and mocked him. Herod then sent Jesus back to Pilate. Although Herod and Pilate had been enemies, they became friends on that very day.

Pilate Seeks to Release Jesus
Luke 23:13-25; John 18:39-19:16;
Matthew 27:15-26; Mark 15:6-15-20

Pilate called together the chief priests, and the rulers, and the people, and said to them, "You have brought me this man as one who was misleading the people. And after examining him before you, behold, I did not find this man guilty of any of your charges against him. Neither did Herod, for he sent him back to us. Look, nothing deserving death has been done by him. I will therefore punish and release him." ᴱˢⱽ

At the Passover feast the governor was accustomed to releasing one prisoner whom the people would choose. At that time, they had a notorious prisoner called Barabbas, who was a robber, insurrectionist, and murderer. Pilate said to the people, "Whom do you want me to release to you? Barabbas or Jesus?" For he knew that they had handed Jesus over because of envy.

Pilate's wife sent a message to him, saying, "Have nothing to do with that just man, for I have suffered many things today in a dream because of him."

But the chief priests and elders persuaded the people to ask for Barabbas and destroy Jesus. Pilate said, "What then shall I do with Jesus who is called Christ?" They all said to him, "Let him be crucified!" Then the governor said, "Why? What evil has he done?" But they cried even more loudly, saying, "Let him be crucified."

When Pilate saw that he could not prevail, but that a tumult was rising, he took water and washed his hands before the people, saying, "I am innocent of the blood of this just person. You see to it." All the people answered, "His blood be on us and on our children."

Then he released Barabbas to them; and he had Jesus scourged. The soldiers made a crown of thorns and put it on his head, and they put a purple robe on him. They mocked him, saying, "Hail, King of the Jews!" And they struck him with their hands.

Pilate said to the people, "Behold, I am bringing him out to you, that you may know that I find no fault in him." Then Jesus came out, wearing the crown of thorns and the purple robe. And Pilate said to them, "Behold the Man!" See Jesus in his weakened condition; blood was covering his face from the crown of thorns! This may have been Pilate's last effort to appease the Jews and spare the life of Jesus.

But when the chief priests and officers saw him, they cried out, "Crucify him, crucify him!" Pilate said, "You take him and crucify him, for I find no fault in him."

The Jews replied, "We have a law, and according to our law he ought to die, because he made himself the Son of God."

Therefore, when Pilate heard that saying, he was even more afraid. He went again into his headquarters with Jesus and asked him, "Where are you from?" But Jesus did not answer. Then Pilate said to him, "Are you not speaking to me? Do you not know that I have power to crucify you, and power to release you?" Jesus answered, "You could have no power at all against me unless it had been given you from above. Therefore, the one who delivered me to you has the greater sin."

From then on Pilate sought to release him, but the Jews said, "If you let this man go, you are not Caesar's friend. Whoever makes himself a king speaks against Caesar."

When Pilate heard this, he brought Jesus out, and he sat down on the judgment seat and said to them, "Shall I crucify your King?" The chief priest answered, "We have no king but Caesar!" Pilate then delivered Jesus to the Jews to be crucified. ^{John} After the Roman soldiers had mocked Jesus, they took the purple robe off him, put his own clothes on him, and led him out to crucify him.
Mark

NOTES

The Crucifixion and Burial

Bearing the Cross
John 19:17; Luke 23:26-33;
Matthew 27:31-33; Mark 15:21-22

Jesus bearing his cross went out to a place called the Place of a Skull, which is called in the Hebrew, Golgotha; and in the Latin it is called Calvary. And as they led Jesus away, they compelled Simon of Cyrene to bear the cross after Jesus. In his weakened condition from the beatings and scourging, Jesus apparently was not able to bear it. Mark describes Simon as the father of Alexander and Rufus, indicating that they were well-known disciples. And a great crowd of people followed Jesus, and women cried and mourned for him. But Jesus turned and said to them, "Daughters of Jerusalem, do not weep for me, but weep for yourselves and for your children. For indeed the days are coming in which they will say, 'Blessed are the barren, wombs that never bore, and breasts which never nursed!' Then they will begin to say to the mountains, 'Fall on us!' and to the hills, 'Cover us!'" When they had come to the place called Calvary, there they crucified him with two others, one on either side, and Jesus in the center.

The Crucifixion of Jesus
Mark 15:23-28; Matthew 27:34, 37-38;
Luke 23:33, 34, 38; John 19:17-22

To prepare him for the crucifixion, they offered Jesus wine mingled with myrrh (gall) to diminish the pain, but he refused it. Jesus was crucified at "the third hour," our nine o'clock in the morning. Pilate wrote a title in Hebrew, Greek, and Latin, and put it on the cross, which read: "JESUS OF NAZARETH, THE KING OF THE JEWS." They also crucified two robbers, one on his right and the other on his left. The Scripture was fulfilled which says, "And he was numbered with the transgressors." (Isaiah 53:12) Then Jesus prayed, "Father forgive them, for they do not know what they do."

The Soldiers Divide His Clothing
John 19:23-24; Matthew 27:35-36;
Mark 15:24; Luke 23:34

When they had crucified Jesus, the soldiers divided his garments into four parts, with each soldier receiving a part. There was also a tunic without seam, woven from the top to the bottom in one piece. They said, "Let us cast lots for it, whose it shall be," that the Scripture might be fulfilled which says, "They divided my garments among them, and for my clothing they cast lots." (Psalm 22:18)

Jesus Is Mocked while on the Cross
Luke 23:35-37; Matthew 27:39-44; Mark 15:29-32

Those who passed by reviled Jesus, wagging their heads, and saying, "You who destroys the temple and in three days builds it, save yourself. If you are the Son of God come down from the cross." The chief priests with the scribes and elders also mocked him, saying, "He saved others; himself he cannot save. If he is the King of Israel, let him now come down from the cross, and we will believe. He trusted in God, let him deliver him now, if he will have him; for he said, 'I am the Son of God.'" Even the robbers who were crucified with him reviled him in the same way. The soldiers also mocked him, saying, "If you are the King of the Jews, save yourself." This fulfilled the prophecy of Psalm 22:7-8, which says, "All who see me mock me; they hurl insults, shaking their heads: 'He trusts in the LORD; let the LORD rescue him. Let him deliver him, since he delights in him.'" NIV

Jesus Provides for His Mother
John 19:25-27

Mary the mother of Jesus was standing by the cross with John and some women who were followers of Jesus. When Jesus saw his mother, he said to her, "Woman, behold your son." John refers to himself as "the disciple whom Jesus loved." (John 21:20) And Jesus said to John, "Behold, your mother." And from that hour, John took Mary to his own home.

One of the Thieves Repents
Luke 23:39-43

Then one of the criminals who were crucified hurled insults at Jesus, saying, "If you are the Christ, save yourself and us." But the other thief rebuked him and said, "Do you not fear God, seeing you are in the same condemnation? And we indeed justly, for we receive the due reward of our deeds; but this man has done nothing wrong."

And he said to Jesus, "Lord, remember me when you come into your kingdom." Jesus said to him, "Truly, I say to you, today you shall be with me in Paradise." This penitent thief must have known something about Jesus and his teachings, because he believed that the kingdom of Jesus was yet to come. The conduct of Jesus during his humiliation and great sufferings must have caused this man to believe that Jesus is the Christ, the Son of God. He asked the other thief, "Do you not fear God?"

Jesus Suffers Alone in Darkness
Luke 23:44-45;
Matthew 27:45-49; Mark 15:33-36; John 19:28-29

There was darkness over all the land from the sixth hour (our twelve noon) until the ninth hour (our 3 p.m.). Jesus was in darkness for three hours suffering alone. When the sunlight returned at 3 p.m., Jesus cried out with a loud voice so all could hear, "My God, My God, why have you forsaken me?" These are the opening words of Psalm 22. Jesus quoted these words to let everyone know that he had fulfilled the prophecies of this psalm. He had suffered alone. He had been ridiculed, despised, and mocked by the people. They had pierced his hands and feet. They had cast lots for his clothing. Jesus knowing that all things were accomplished, and that the Scripture might be fulfilled said, "I thirst." This is another prophecy of Psalm 22. They filled a sponge with vinegar and put it on hyssop, and put it to his mouth. "My strength is dried up like a potsherd; and my tongue cleaves to my jaws; and you have brought me into the dust of death." (Psalm 22:15)

Jesus Dies on the Cross
John 19:30;
Luke 23:46; Mark 15:37

Having received the vinegar, Jesus said, "It is finished." He had completed the work the Father had sent him to do. Jesus shouted with a loud voice, "Father, into your hands I commit my spirit." Having said this, he gave up his spirit and died. Jesus voluntarily gave up his life. He had said concerning his life, "No man takes it from me, but I lay it down of myself." (John 10:18) The fact that he was able to shout his last words is proof that he did not die of exhaustion due to the crucifixion. Those crucified normally died of exhaustion after days on the cross.

Miraculous Signs at His Death
Luke 23:47-49;
Matthew 27:50-56; Mark 15:38-41

When the centurion saw this, he glorified God, saying, "Certainly this was a righteous man!" All the people that came to that sight, beholding the things that were done, smote their breasts and left. Those who were personally acquainted with Jesus and the women who followed him from Galilee stood at a distance, beholding these things. Among them were Mary Magdalene and

Mary the mother of James the less and of Joses, and Salome, the mother of Zebedee's children. These women had ministered to Jesus in Galilee.

When Jesus died, the veil of the temple was torn in two from the top to the bottom; and the earth quaked, and the rocks were split, and graves were opened, and many bodies of the saints who had died were raised. When the centurion and those with him saw these things, they feared God greatly, saying, "Truly this was the Son of God."

A Soldier Pierced Jesus' Side
John 19:31-37

The next day was the Passover. And because the Jews did not want the crucified bodies to remain on a cross on this special holy day of rest (Exodus 12:16), they requested that their legs might be broken to cause their death. (Those crucified had to push up with their legs to take a breath.) When the soldiers came to Jesus, they found that he was already dead; therefore, they did not break his legs. Jesus died as the Passover Lamb to take away the sin of the world. (John 1:29) Not one bone of the Passover lamb was to be broken. (Exodus 12:43-46) To make sure that Jesus was dead, a soldier with a spear pierced his side, and blood and water flowed forth. This fulfilled the prophecies of Zechariah 12:10 and 13:1. The apostle John was an eye-witness to these things.

The Burial of Jesus
Matthew 27:57-60; Mark 15:42-46;
Luke 23:50-52; John 19:38

When evening came, Joseph of Arimathea, went to Pilate and asked permission to bury the body of Jesus. Joseph was a rich man and a prominent member of the Sanhedrin; however, he had not consented to the death of Jesus. Joseph was a disciple of Jesus and was waiting for the kingdom of God. Nicodemus, also a Jewish ruler who believed in Jesus (John 3:1), joined Joseph in wrapping the body in linen with a mixture of myrrh and aloes. They buried the body of Jesus in Joseph's own new tomb in a garden near the place where Jesus was crucified. A stone was rolled to cover the entrance to the tomb.

The Women Behold the Tomb
Luke 23:54-56; Mark 15:47; Matthew 27:61

The women who had ministered to Jesus in Galilee, saw the tomb where the body of Jesus was laid. They returned to their homes to prepare spices and ointments for his body, and they waited until after the sabbath. Among the women were Mary Magdalene and Mary the mother of Joses.

Pilate Sets a Guard at the Tomb
Matthew 27:62-66

The day after the Day of Preparation for the Passover began at sundown on Thursday. The chief priests (who were Sadducees) and the Pharisees went to Pilate requesting that he give the command to make the tomb secure until the third day, so Jesus' disciples could not steal his body and claim that he had been raised from the dead. Pilate authorized the use of a Roman guard to make it as secure as possible. The stone was sealed with the Roman seal, and Roman soldiers guarded the tomb.

The Resurrection and Ascension

Jesus Is Raised from the Dead
Matthew 28:1-4

After the end of the sabbaths[44] (the Passover and the seventh day), Jesus rose from the dead early on Sunday, the first day of the week. While it was still dark, just as it began to dawn, there was a great earthquake. An angel of the Lord descended from heaven and rolled back the stone from the door of the tomb; and he sat upon it. His face was shining brightly and his clothing was white as snow. The soldiers became afraid. They began shaking with fear and became as dead men. Jesus came back to life, and he left the tomb.

Women Come to the Tomb
Mark 16:1-4; Luke 24:1-2

Early Sunday morning as it began to dawn, the women who had ministered to Jesus in Galilee bought spices to anoint his body. As they were approaching the tomb, they were discussing who would roll away the stone for them. To their surprise when they saw the tomb, the great stone had been rolled away. Mary Magdalene was among the women who had come to the tomb.

Mary Magdalene Tells Peter and John
John 20:1-2

When Mary Magdalene saw that the stone had been removed from the door of the tomb, she thought that the soldiers had removed the body of Jesus to another place. She ran and told Peter and John, "They have taken away the Lord out of the tomb, and we do not know where they have laid him." RSV

---

[44] The Greek word translated "sabbath" in Matthew 28:1 is genitive plural.

The Women Enter the Tomb
Luke 24:3-11; Mark 16:5-8; Matthew 28:5-8

After Mary Magdalene left the other women at the tomb, they entered the tomb and did not see the body of Jesus. As they were perplexed and wondering what had happened, two angels appeared to them, saying, "Why do you seek the living among the dead?" Matthew and Mark mention the angel who said to them, "Be not afraid. You seek Jesus of Nazareth, who was crucified. He is risen; he is not here. Come, see the place where the Lord lay." The angel told them to tell the disciples Jesus is risen from the dead, and they would see him in Galilee. The women left the tomb filled with great joy; and they went to report these things to the disciples, but they did not believe it.

The Empty Tomb
John 20:3-10; Luke 24:12

After the women had left, Peter and John ran to the tomb along with Mary Magdalene following. John got there first. And looking in, he saw the linen clothes lying; but he did enter. Then Peter came and went into the tomb. He saw the linen clothes and the napkin that had been about his head wrapped in a place by itself. Jesus had removed the grave clothes and had neatly arranged them. He had taken his time to leave the empty tomb. If someone had stolen his body, they would have taken it still wrapped in the linen cloths with the napkin about the head. When John entered the tomb and saw these things, he believed. Then Peter and John left the tomb and returned home.

Jesus Appears to Mary Magdalene
John 20:11-18; Mark 16:9-11

But Mary stood outside the tomb weeping. As she wept, she looked into the tomb and saw two angels. And they said to her, "Woman, why are you weeping?" She said, "Because they have taken away my Lord, and I do not know where they have laid him." Then she turned around and saw Jesus standing; but in her sadness, she did not recognize him and turned back toward the tomb. Jesus asked her, "Woman, why are you weeping? Whom do you seek?" Supposing he was the gardener she said, "Sir, if you have taken him from here, tell me where you have laid him." Jesus said to her, "Mary." She recognized his voice; and turning around she said to him, "Master!"

Jesus told Mary to stop clinging to him, because he had not yet ascended to his Father. The verb translated "touch" in the KJV also means "fasten to, adhere to, cling to;" [45] and it is in the present imperative mood, a command which indicates continued action. He would no longer be with her and his other disciples as before; things would be different. Before Jesus ascended to the Father, he would appear to them and then vanish. Jesus' first appearance was to Mary Magdalene, according to Mark 16:9. She told his disciples she had seen Jesus alive; but they did not believe it.

Jesus Appears to the Women on the Road
Matthew 28:9-10

While the other women were on their way to tell the angel's message to the disciples, Jesus appeared to them. They came and held him by the feet and worshiped him. He said to them. "Be not afraid. Go tell my brethren to go into Galilee, and they shall see me there."

The Guard's Report to the Chief Priests
Matthew 28:11-15

Some of the soldiers that had been watching the tomb reported to the chief priests all that had happened. The Jews bribed the soldiers with a large sum of money to say that Jesus' disciples came by night and stole the body while they slept. Sleeping while on duty and

---

[45] Joseph Henry Thayer, *Greek-English Lexicon of the N.T.*, p. 70

allowing the Roman seal of the tomb to be broken were punishable by death. So, the Jews assured the soldiers that they would also bribe the governor if he heard about this. The Jews still explain the empty tomb with this lie.

Jesus on the Road to Emmaus
Luke 24:13-35; Mark 16:12-13

The same day, two disciples were walking to a village called Emmaus, that was seven miles from Jerusalem. Jesus came near and began walking with them, but they were kept from recognizing him. Mark explains why they did not recognize Jesus at first: "He appeared in another form" to them while they were walking. They told him about Jesus of Nazareth, who had been crucified; and they had hoped that he was the one who would redeem Israel. They also told him about the women and others finding his tomb empty earlier that day.

Then Jesus said to them, "O foolish ones, and slow of heart to believe in all that the prophets have spoken! Ought not the Christ to have suffered these things and to enter into His glory?" NKJV Then he taught them all that Moses and the Prophets had written about the Christ.

When they came near to Emmaus, the disciples invited Jesus to eat with them. As Jesus blessed the bread and gave it to them, they could see that he was Jesus, but he quickly vanished from their sight.

These two disciples returned to Jerusalem to tell the apostles what had happened on the road and how they recognized Jesus when he gave thanks for their food. The apostles said, "It is true! The Lord has risen and has appeared to Simon" (Peter).

Jesus Appears to the Disciples on Sunday
Luke 24:44-43; Mark 16:14-18; John 20:19-23

While they said these things, Jesus stood in their midst and said, "Peace to you!" But they were terrified and frightened, supposing they had seen a spirit, because the doors were shut. Jesus said to them, "Why are you troubled? And why do doubts arise in your hearts? Look at my hands and my feet, that it is I myself. Handle me and see, for a spirit does not have flesh and bones as you see I have." They wondered, and they still did not believe for joy. ^{Luke}

Jesus rebuked them for their unbelief and hardness of heart, because they did not believe those who had seen him after he had risen. ^{Mark}

Jesus then asked, "Do you have any food here?" They had just eaten. (Mark 16:14) So, they gave him a piece of a broiled fish and some honeycomb. And he ate in in their presence. (Luke 24:43)

Jesus then gave the great commission to his apostles for the first time, "Go into all the world and proclaim the gospel to the whole creation. Whoever believes and is baptized will be saved; but whoever does not believe will be condemned. And these signs will accompany those who believe: in my name they shall cast out demons; they shall speak in new tongues; they will pick up serpents with their hands; and if they drink any deadly poison, it will not hurt them; they will lay their hands on the sick, and they will recover." ^{ESV} (Mark 16:15-18)

Jesus said to them again, "Peace to you! As the Father has sent me, I also send you." He breathed on them and said, "Receive the Holy Spirit. If you forgive the sins of any, they are forgiven them; if you retain the sins of any, they are retained." (John 20:21-23)

Jesus Appears to Thomas
John 20:24-29

Thomas was not with the other apostles when Jesus appeared to them on the day of his resurrection. He said, "Unless I shall see in his hands the print of the nails, and put my finger into the print of the nails, and thrust my hand into his side, I will not believe."

Jesus appeared a week later to his apostles. ᴺᴵⱽ A week was called eight days. This second appearance was also on a Sunday. This time Thomas was with them; and the doors were shut as before. Jesus stood in their midst and said, "Peace be to you."

Then he said to Thomas, "Put your finger here; see my hands. Reach out your hand and put it into my side. Stop doubting and believe." ᴺᴵⱽ

And Thomas said to Jesus, "My Lord and my God." He replied, "Thomas, because you have seen me, you have believed; blessed are they that have not seen, and yet have believed."

Proof that Jesus is the Christ, the Son of God
John 20:30-31

Jesus did many other miraculous signs in the presence of his disciples, which are not written in John's account of the good news. But John has given us sufficient evidence to believe that Jesus is the Christ, the Son of God; and as we believe, we may have life through his name.

Jesus Appears at the Sea of Galilee
John 21:1-14

After the Feast of Unleavened Bread, the disciples returned to their homes on the shores of the Sea of Galilee, which is also known as the Sea of Tiberias. Peter said, "I am going fishing." Thomas, Nathanael, James, John, and two other disciples replied, "We are going with you." They fished all night and caught nothing.

When morning came, Jesus stood on the shore, but the disciples did not recognize him at first. Jesus called out to them, "Children, have you any fish?" And they answered, "No." He said to them, "Cast the net on the right side of the boat, and you will find some." When they did this, they were not able to draw the net in because of the great catch. John said, "It is the Lord!" When Peter heard it was the Lord, he jumped into the water to go to Jesus. The other disciples came in the boat, dragging the net full of one hundred and fifty-three fish.

As soon as they came to shore, they saw a fire of hot coals with a breakfast of fish and bread prepared for them. Jesus said, "Come and dine." This was the third time Jesus appeared to his disciples after his resurrection.

Jesus Restores Peter
John 21:15-17

Peter had denied Jesus three times; now Jesus is asking him to confess him three times. He asked, "Simon, son of John, do you love me more than these?" Peter answered, "Yes, Lord, you know that I love you." Jesus said, "Feed my lambs." He said to him a second time, "Simon, son of John, do you love me?" Peter said to him, "Yes, Lord, you know that I love you." Jesus said, "Feed my sheep." Jesus said to him the third time, "Simon, son of John, do you love me?" Peter replied, "Lord, you know all things, you know that I love you." Jesus said, "Feed my sheep."

Peter was grieved when Jesus asked him to confess his love three times, because this surely reminded him that he had denied Jesus three times. Peter had failed to believe Jesus when warned that he would deny him three times. He had said, "Even if all fall away, I will not" (Mark 14:29); and "Lord, I am ready to go with you, both to prison and to death." (Luke 22:34). Peter now confesses, "Lord, you know all things." Peter is a changed man; he would humbly trust the knowledge and authority of Jesus.

Peter obeyed Jesus and fed his sheep. He confessed him on the Day of Pentecost, saying "Know assuredly that God has made this Jesus ... both Lord and Christ." (Acts 2:38) "His divine power has given us all things that pertain to life and godliness." (2 Peter 1:3) Peter's last recorded words to Christians are for them to "grow in the grace and knowledge of our Lord and Savior Jesus Christ. To him be the glory both now and forever. Amen." (2 Peter 3:18)

Jesus Predicts Peter's Death
John 21:18-19

When Peter was young, he was free to do as he pleased; but Jesus said to him, "When you are old, you will stretch out your hands, and another will gird you and carry you where you do not wish." ^{NKJV} This signified by what death he would glorify God—he would be crucified. Early church history records that in AD 68, Peter was crucified by Nero in Rome. The gospel of John was written many years after Peter's martyrdom.

Peter would be given the opportunity to show his love for Jesus by going to prison and to death. Peter had said that he would do these things for Jesus in Luke 22:34. He would be given the chance to prove his love.

Then Jesus said to Peter, "Follow me." Peter began to literally follow Jesus as he walked away. Peter turned and noticed that John was following him. So, he asked Jesus what John would do. Jesus said, "If I want him to remain until I come, what is that to you? You follow me." ^{NASB} Peter then understood that Jesus wanted him to follow his spiritual example, no matter what others might do.

Some misunderstood what Jesus said concerning John; they thought that John would not die before Jesus would come again. John corrects this false interpretation.

It was none of Peter's business what would happen to John. He was to follow Jesus. We should not compare ourselves with others. (2 Cor. 10:12) John would out live all of the other apostles. Although he was exiled to the island of Patmos for preaching the gospel of Christ, he lived a long life and did not die the death of a martyr.

The Testimony of the Elders at Ephesus
John 21:24

John was living in Ephesus when he wrote his account of the life of Christ. The testimony in this verse is thought to be the words of the elders at Ephesus; notice the "**we**" statement in the verse. "This is the disciple who testifies of these things and wrote these things; and **we know** that his testimony is true." Other writers wrote these words about John.

Jesus Appears on a Mountain in Galilee
Matthew 28:16-20

The apostles went to a mountain in Galilee which Jesus had appointed for them. It is believed that this is when Jesus "was seen by over five hundred brethren at once," mentioned by Paul in 1 Corinthians 15:6. And when they saw Jesus, they worshiped him; but some doubted.

Jesus said to them, "All authority has been given to Me in heaven and on earth. Go therefore and make disciples of all the nations, baptizing them in the name of the Father and of the Son and of the Holy Spirit, teaching them to observe all things that I have commanded you; and lo, I am with you always, even to the end of the age." NKJV This is the second Great Commission of Jesus.

The Third Commission of Jesus
Luke 24:44-49; Acts 1:1-8

The apostles had returned to Jerusalem a few days before the Day of Pentecost. Jesus had presented himself alive after his death by many infallible proofs, being seen by his apostles during forty days and speaking to them of things pertaining to the kingdom of God.

Being assembled with his apostles Jesus said, "These are the words which I spoke to you, while I was yet with you, that all things must be fulfilled, which were written in the law of Moses, and in the prophets, and in the psalms, concerning me." Then he opened their understanding, and he said, to them, "Thus it is written, and thus it behooved Christ to suffer, and to rise from the dead the third day. And that **repentance and remission of sins should be preached in his name among all nations** beginning at Jerusalem. And you are witnesses of these things. Behold, I send **the promise** of my Father upon you." The promise that Jesus is referring to is the promise God had made to Abraham in Genesis 22:18, "In your seed (Christ) all the nations of the earth shall be blessed." This became the theme of the Bible. (Read Galatians 3:7-29.) Peter also mentioned this promise in Acts 2:39.

Jesus commanded the apostles to stay in the city of Jerusalem until they were given power from on high. He said, "John baptized with water, but you shall be baptized with the Holy Spirit not many days from now." NKJV

The apostles asked Jesus, "Lord, will you at this time restore again the kingdom to Israel?" They were still thinking that the kingdom of God would be an earthly physical kingdom. Jesus said, "It is not for you to know the times or the seasons, which the Father has put in his own power. But you will receive power when the Holy Spirit comes upon you. And you shall be witnesses to me both in Jerusalem, and in Samaria, and to the ends of the earth." NKJV

The Ascension of Jesus
Luke 24:50-51; Acts 1:9-11, Mark 16:19

Jesus led the apostles out of Jerusalem as far as Bethany on the Mount of Olives, and he lifted up his hands and blessed them. While he blessed them, he was taken up and carried into heaven. A cloud received him out of their sight. And while they looked steadfastly toward heaven as he went up, behold two angels stood by them and said, "Men of Galilee, why do you stand gazing up into heaven? This same Jesus who was taken up from you into heaven, will so come in like manner as you saw him go into heaven." Jesus was received up into heaven, and he sat down on the right hand of God.

The Response of the Apostles
Luke 24:52-53; Mark 16:20

After worshiping Jesus, the apostles returned to Jerusalem with great joy. They were continually in the temple, praising God.

And the apostles went forth and preached everywhere, the Lord working with them and confirming the word with signs following. Amen.

John's Closing Statement
John 21:25

"And there are also many other things which Jesus did, which if they should be written every one, I suppose that even the world itself could not contain the books that should be written. Amen."

Bibliography

Ash, Anthony Lee, ***The Gospel According to Luke, Parts 1 & 2***
The Living Word Commentary. Austin, Texas:
Sweet Publishing Company, 1972 and 1973

Barclay, William, ***The Gospel of Luke.*** Philadelphia,
Pennsylvania: The Westminster Press, 1956

Coffman, James Burton, ***Mark.*** Coffman's Bible Commentary.
Austin, Texas: Firm Foundation Publishing House.

Earle, Ralph, ***Exploring the New Testament.*** Kansas City,
Missouri: Beacon Hill Press, 1959

Jenkins, W. L., ***The Westminster Historical Atlas of the Bible, Revised Edition.*** Philadelphia, Pennsylvania:
The Westminster Press, 1956

Johnson, B. W., ***The People's New Testament.*** Nashville,
Tennessee: Gospel Advocate Company, 1990

Kent, Homer L, Jr., ***Matthew.*** The Wycliffe Bible Commentary.
Nashville, Tennessee: The Southwestern Publishing Company,
1962

Lewis, Jack P., ***The Gospel According to Matthew, Parts 1 & 2.***
The Living Word Commentary. Austin, Texas:
Sweet Publishing Company, 1976

Maier, Paul L., ***Eusebius—The Church History.*** Grand Rapids,
Michigan: Kregel Publications, 1999

McGarvey, J, W., ***Matthew and Mark.*** Cincinnati, Ohio:
Central Book Concern, 1879

McMillan, Earle, ***The Gospel According to Mark.*** The Living
Word Commentary. Austin, Texas: Sweet Publishing
Company, 1973

Pack, Frank, ***The Gospel According to John, Parts 1 & 2.***
The Living Word Commentary. Austin, Texas:
Sweet Publishing Company, 1975 and 1977

Peloubet, F.N., ***Peloubet's Bible Dictionary.*** Philadelphia, Pennsylvania: The John C. Winston Company, 1947

Roberts, J. W., ***The Letters of John.***
The Living Word Commentary. Austin, Texas: Sweet Publishing Company, 1968

Roper, David L., ***The Life of Christ, 1 & 2.***
Truth for Today Commentary. Searcy, Arkansas: Resource Publications, 2003

Smith, F. LaGard, ***The Narrated Bible.*** Eugene, Oregon Harvest House Publishers, 1984

Tenney, Merrill C., ***New Testament Survey.*** Grand Rapids, Michigan: Wm. B. Eerdmans Publishing Co., 1961

Thayer, Joseph Henry, ***Thayer's Greek-English Lexicon of the New Testament.*** Grand Rapids, Michigan: Zondervan Publishing House, 1970

Wilkinson, Bruce & Boa, Kenneth, ***Talk Thru the Bible.*** Nashville, Tennessee: Thomas Nelson Publishers, 1983